THREE CENTURIES OF

WEDGWOOD

ART, INDUSTRY AND DESIGN

THREE CENTURIES OF
WEDGWOOD

ART, INDUSTRY AND DESIGN

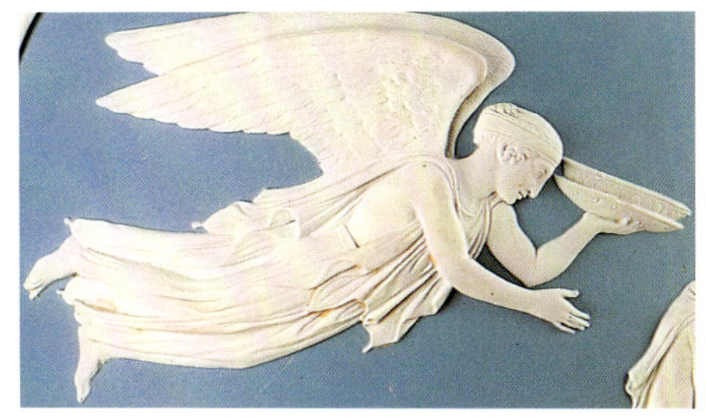

Margaret Legge

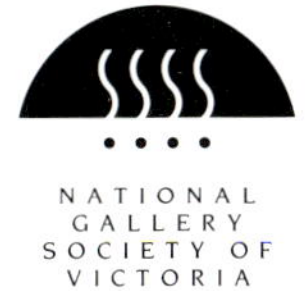

NATIONAL
GALLERY
SOCIETY OF
VICTORIA

National Gallery of Victoria

Published by the National Gallery of Victoria
180 St Kilda Road, Melbourne, Victoria, 3004

National Library of Australia Cataloguing-in-Publication
entry:

Legge, Margaret, 1946–.
    Three centuries of Wedgwood: art, industry and
    design.

    Bibliography.
    ISBN 0 7241 0174 8.

    1. Wedgwood ware - History. 2. Pottery - England -
    Exhibitions. 3. Pottery, English - Exhibitions.
    I. National Gallery of Victoria. II. Title.

738.09410749451

Designer: Jo Waite
Editor: Margot Holden
Wordprocessor: Judy Shelverton
Printer: Buscombe Printers
Photography: Garry Sommerfeld

CONTENTS

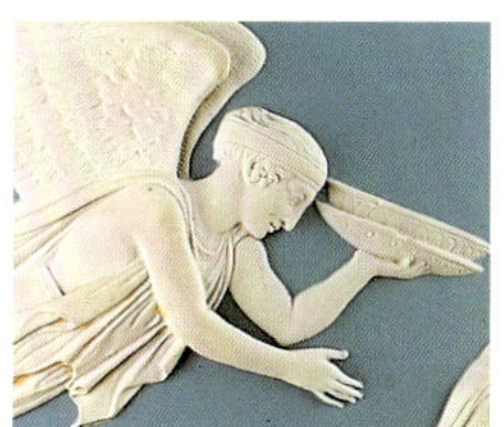

ACKNOWLEDGEMENTS

This catalogue is the result of a long association between Keith and Norma Deutsher and the National Gallery of Victoria. I have been privileged to know them and to learn from their experience for many years; we worked together with the Wedgwood Society of Australia to show 18th century Wedgwood at the Gallery in 1980. The ceramics which they are placing in the Gallery's keeping, the first of which were received in 1992, transform the collection into a special resource and a source of enjoyment for future generations.

The Gallery has collected Wedgwood from its earliest years, commencing with a medallion of Josiah Wedgwood, founder of the factory, which was purchased in 1868 (cat. no. 35). But despite some interesting acquisitions it is only with the Deutshers' gift that the Gallery is at last able to give due emphasis to ceramics made in Josiah's lifetime and to really show the scope of this manufacture which still flourishes today.

I would like to thank the Director James Mollison and Terence Lane, Senior Curator of Australian Art (formerly head of the Department of Decorative Arts), for their support for this publication and the exhibition it will accompany. My appreciation goes to the Gallery staff who have contributed in their specialised roles: Philip

Jago and Jennie Moloney in the Publications Department; Garry Sommerfeld, Photographer; Jo Waite, Designer; and Judy Shelverton whose skills and patience in processing the manuscript are much appreciated. Tom Mosby, Conservator, is to be thanked for his careful preparation of the objects. The editor, Margot Holden, provided valuable help at the crucial time.

My thanks go to The National Gallery Society of Victoria for sponsorship of the catalogue.

The bibliography is hardly sufficient to acknowledge my debt to the various authors, and in particular I would like to mention Aileen Dawson, Alison Kelly, Robin Reilly, Gaye Blake Roberts and Geoffrey Wills, also Maureen Batkin's publication on the later wares. The scope of a catalogue is necessarily limited, but the literature old and new is vast and leads in many directions: I would like to draw particular attention to the letters of Josiah I Wedgwood to his partner Thomas Bentley, many of which have been published by Lady Farrer and by Ann Finer and George Savage. They are a rich historical resource and reveal not only the story of Wedgwood's ceramics but the potter's intelligence and wit, and the breadth of his interest in art, industry, politics, and the moral and scientific issues of his day.

DIRECTOR'S FOREWORD

When in 1990 I accepted an invitation from Keith and Norma Deutsher to view their collection of Wedgwood ceramics I knew that they were ardent and knowledgable collectors, but I was hardly prepared to find in Melbourne, as I did, a large collection of Wedgwood of world importance.

Keith and Norma Deutsher are well known to ceramic collectors. Keith Deutsher developed his interest in Wedgwood as a teenager and has been collecting in earnest since the late 1950s. In 1973 he became the founder and foundation president of the Wedgwood Society of Australia. In this capacity, for thirteen years he worked to further public education concerning the remarkable 18th-century potter Josiah Wedgwood and his famous and enduring factory. In 1988 he was appointed an honorary member of the Board of Governors of the Wedgwood International Seminar based in New York. He has also been a member of the Wedgwood Society of New York.

The Deutshers have long shared their interest in Wedgwood with others, from the most modest beginner to the most privileged and knowledgable. They are now progressively giving their important possessions to the National Gallery of Victoria, along with a supporting library on the subject, to further the appreciation and study of Wedgwood in Australia. For this most civilised benefaction, which commenced in 1992, Keith and Norma Deutsher were awarded Life Membership of the Gallery in 1993.

The Deutshers have collected rare and important works of the early Wedgwood & Bentley period, as well as key pieces from the later 18th century, including two quite different First Edition examples of the Portland vase, and major works of later date. The present catalogue describes their gifts and promised gifts to the Gallery, augmented by items from the Gallery's earlier holdings in order to document as broadly as possible the heritage of Wedgwood.

James Mollison AO
Director, National Gallery of Victoria

A BRIEF HISTORY OF WEDGWOOD

Josiah Wedgwood, founder of the distinguished factory which bears his name, was born in 1730 into a family of potters working at Burslem, one of a group of small pottery-producing towns in north Staffordshire which have since merged within the municipality of Stoke-on-Trent.

The local pottery industry of this region emerges into the light of history at the end of the 17th century.[1] At that time it was a poor area, unsuited to agriculture, but well supplied with workable clay and coal to fire its kilns (at a time when wood fuel was in short supply). In the first half of the 18th century it developed a number of fine earthenwares of a quality suitable for sale to

a broader market, including fashionable London.

By the middle of the 18th century the main types of Staffordshire pottery, among several colours and styles, were creamware (a refined earthenware finished with a lead-based glaze), and white salt-glazed stoneware.[2] Both were made using white clay brought from Dorset or Devon[3] and calcined flint[4] to temper the clay, the salt-glaze being fired at a higher temperature.

The Staffordshire potters competed against the tin-glazed, mainly blue and white, earthenware known as 'delftware' and against the luxury product, porcelain, which was still mostly imported from China[5] but was produced soon after 1750 in commercial quantities at Chelsea, Bow, Derby, Worcester and other centres.

They produced a variety of tablewares such as mugs and plates, but their best pottery was required above all for the new fashion of taking tea: Rococo-style teapots were made in moulded salt-glazed stoneware, and in a creamware body with trailing vines in relief and naturalistic branch handles, decorated with mottled lead glazes like tortoiseshell. Red wares were also made, sometimes applied with 'sprigged' reliefs of white clay and glazed. There were also unglazed black wares called 'black Egyptian'. 'Agate' wares were made in imitation of figured stone by wedging different-coloured clays together to form a swirled pattern.

The early Staffordshire potteries were, typically, small-scale workshops and family-run, like the Churchyard Pottery in Burslem which was passed down through generations of Wedgwoods from the middle of the 17th century

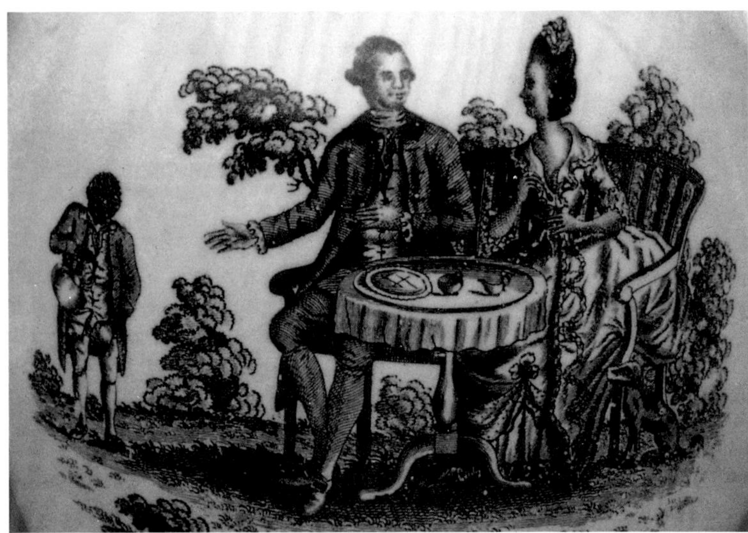

Detail of Wedgwood teapot printed wih 'Tea party' pattern by Sadler & Green of Liverpool (cat. no. 2).

before Josiah Wedgwood was apprenticed to his brother Thomas in 1744. Josiah was fourteen years old and had received a scant three years of formal schooling.

He acquired the basic skills of a potter within the context of this small family business, but his apprenticeship was cut short by an attack of smallpox. He is next recorded in 1752 as a partner in a pottery at Cliff Bank, Stoke, run by Harrison and Alders, but nothing is known of its production.

He then formed an important partnership with Thomas Whieldon (1719–95) at nearby Fenton Vivian, which lasted from 1754 to 1759. Whieldon was the leading Staffordshire potter of his day, producing the tortoiseshell-glazed, salt-glazed and agate wares which were in general use. It is a measure of Whieldon's stature that the major potters of the later 18th century, Josiah Spode and William Greatbatch, also worked for him in their youth.[6]

During his time with Whieldon, Wedgwood made experiments which remained his own property at the dissolution of the partnership. The most notable of these involved an improved green glaze used on wares moulded in the shape of cauliflowers, pineapples and melons. Typical of the playful naturalism of Rococo taste, these characteristic wares of the Wedgwood–Whieldon period continued to find favour into the mid–1760s.

The partnership may have overlapped Wedgwood's own business which he set up in rented buildings at Ivy House, Burslem, in 1759. There is at present insufficient evidence to separate Whieldon–Wedgwood wares (which differ from Whieldon's salt-glazed, tortoiseshell and creamwares made at the earlier site of Fenton Low[7]) into items made at Fenton Vivian and works from Ivy House. To complicate the story further, Wedgwood was supplied with green-glazed wares by Greatbatch, most likely according to Wedgwood's own recipe.[8] In any case contemporaries knew him as a maker of 'Colly flower ware'[9] (see cat. no. 1).

In 1763, three years after setting up the Ivy House works at Burslem, Wedgwood rented the nearby Brick House works to accommodate his expanded business. This was also called the Bell Works for the belfry he set up to summon his employees (since only the wealthy had clocks or watches). The factory remained active until 1772. His cousin Thomas Wedgwood, having joined him as a journeyman[10] at Ivy House in 1759, became his partner in 1766, and shared the profits of the 'useful wares' made at the Burslem works, and, after 1772 at the Etruria works, until his death in 1788.

The major innovation of Wedgwood's early Burslem factory was an improved creamware body developed in 1763. Creamware was fired at a lower temperature than the salt-glazed stonewares, thereby saving on fuel, and it was less liable to break or chip than other low-fired wares. Attractive, durable and cheap, it was destined to replace salt-glazed and tin-glazed tablewares both in English and in Continental markets.

In 1765 Queen Charlotte wished for a creamware tea service to be decorated with green flowers on a gold ground.[11] The order eventually went to Wedgwood who grasped the opportunity to make an impression where it counted in the world of fashion and submitted also a box of patterns and some vases. By the summer of 1766 Wedgwood had been appointed 'Potter to Her Majesty', and the creamware body had been named Queen's Ware. He set up a London showroom in Mayfair and acquired the services of an agent, William Cox. In 1767 he wrote of presenting constantly changing displays of tablewares to amuse 'my Ladys [who] come in very large Shoals together'.[12]

The Burslem period also saw Wedgwood introduce the use of engine-turning for decoration, previously unknown on pottery. This involved a lathe which incorporated two cams, the 'rose' and the 'crown', that allowed the spinning pot to move in a regular but complex pattern both across and along its axis, while the cutting tool was held steady. It was capable of producing vertical fluting and other elaborate patterns which appear on early Wedgwood pieces (see cat. nos. 26, 27, 54).

Another a great innovation was the practice of sending out creamware to be decorated with transfer prints by Sadler & Green of Liverpool, the first record of this being a bill dated 1761 (see cat. no. 2). This development is an early example of the methods of mass production which arose in 18th-century England and formed the basis of the Industrial Revolution.

At this period Wedgwood also involved himself in the improvement of transport by promoting the construction of turnpike roads (toll roads for which Parliament passed a Bill in 1763) and the Grand Trunk Canal (built 1766–77), designed to link the potteries on the River Trent with the port of Liverpool on the Mersey. In 1766 Wedgwood was elected treasurer of the 'Navigation from the Trent to the Mersey', working alongside the Duke of Bridgewater. Without such undertakings, the Staffordshire pottery could hardly have managed to transport raw materials cheaply or divide the processes of production between different localities with any measure of efficiency. Nor could large quantities of pottery have reached more than a local market.

THE WEDGWOOD AND BENTLEY PARTNERSHIP 1769–80

In 1762 Wedgwood met Thomas Bentley (1730–80), a Liverpool merchant in the wool and cotton trade. Their warm friendship was one of the most important influences on Wedgwood's career and led, in 1769, to the formation of a partnership for the production of a radically new type of pottery.

Born in Derbyshire in 1730, Bentley was a cultivated man with antiquarian interests, though he had left his studies at fifteen or sixteen to be apprenticed to a merchant in Manchester. Like the gentry of the day he had travelled on the Continent, and had a knowledge of languages. He was a prominent citizen of Liverpool and in 1757 he had been a Trustee of its Warrington Academy, an important provincial centre of intellectual life. He and Wedgwood shared an interest in the canal project.

As the manager of the London end of Wedgwood's business, with its painting studio, warehouse and showrooms, Bentley acted as advisor on matters of taste and fashion and was on good terms with such figures as Sir William Hamilton, Ambassador at Naples and collector of ancient Greek vases, Sir Joshua Reynolds, portrait painter and President of the Royal Academy, and the Birmingham manufacturer of metalware, Matthew Boulton (1728–1809) who was, like Wedgwood, a pioneer of industrial techniques.

Wedgwood and Bentley opened their factory on 13 June 1769. Newly built on the Ridgehouse Estate about two miles from Burslem, it was named 'Etruria' after the Italian region where a great many ancient Greek vases had been found, and where they were thought to have been made.[13] To commemorate the first day of the partnership Josiah Wedgwood himself, with Bentley turning the wheel, threw six vases in 'Etruscan' style. Each was inscribed: *Artes Etruriae Renascuntur* (The arts of Etruria are reborn). The factory's Neoclassical program was explicit from the outset.

Neoclassicism, based on a fresh revival of ancient forms, was the leading style of the day in English architecture and the decorative arts, and one to which Wedgwood was to make a distinctive contribution. He adapted a wide variety of classical forms and motifs, and developed new pottery materials sympathetic to this more severe style which displaced the Rococo.

The leading exponent of the Neoclassical style, as far as decoration was concerned, was the architect Robert Adam (1728–92), of whom a younger contemporary later said: 'To Mr Adam's Taste in the Ornaments of his Buildings and Furniture we stand indebted, in-as-much as Manufacturers of every Kind felt, as it were, the electric power of this Revolution in Art'.[14] (Electricity was the latest scientific discovery, not yet a domestic amenity.) Adam's style was rich but purified of Baroque sculptural excess, and built on the study of antiquity, especially the recent discoveries of ancient Roman paintings at Herculaneum and at Pompeii near Naples. Adam designed all manner of objects down to the smallest details of what we now call interior decoration, and the geometrical precision of these designs was well suited to the mechanical processes introduced by Wedgwood for pottery and by the manufacturer Matthew Boulton for metal products. Moreover, Adam encouraged a sort of vase mania. Wedgwood supplied plaques for Adam fireplaces, and tablets to be set into plaster walls.

Wedgwood built up a library of published antiquities, and had access to major British collections of his day.[15] The handsome volumes devoted to the 'Etruscan' vases of Sir William Hamilton had directly inspired the First Day's vases (see cat. no. 11). He bought many casts after antique sculpture (see cat. no. 17). All were to serve as models for the factory's artists.

In 1775 Wedgwood engaged the services

of the young sculptor John Flaxman (1755–1826),[16] whose father was a dealer in casts in London. Flaxman junior was to become the leading Neoclassical sculptor of his age (see cat. no. 18). His youthful work for Wedgwood already shows a graceful and personal interpretation of the antique, with an emphasis on simplicity and clarity of line which was a hallmark of the Neoclassical style at its purest in the fine arts.

The Wedgwood and Bentley period began by specialising in the improved black stoneware they called 'basalt', after the hard natural stone.[17] It was prized as a matt black which, painted in Wedgwood's 'encaustic' technique, could imitate Greek vases (see cat. no. 46). It was also a material valued as having 'the Appearance of Antique Bronze',[18] and suitable for vases, busts and tablets set into architectural schemes of decoration (see cat. no. 14).

The development of the famous 'blue jasper' body was clearly the result of a desire to reproduce the physical characteristics of antique gems carved in the semi-precious stone.[19] Perhaps Wedgwood also knew of the magnificent relief in white marble on a lapis lazuli ground, which had been installed at Moor Park, Hertfordshire, in 1763 when Adam was enlarging and redecorating it.[20]

In 1774, after numerous systematically recorded experiments, Wedgwood wrote with satisfaction that the new jasper body, a

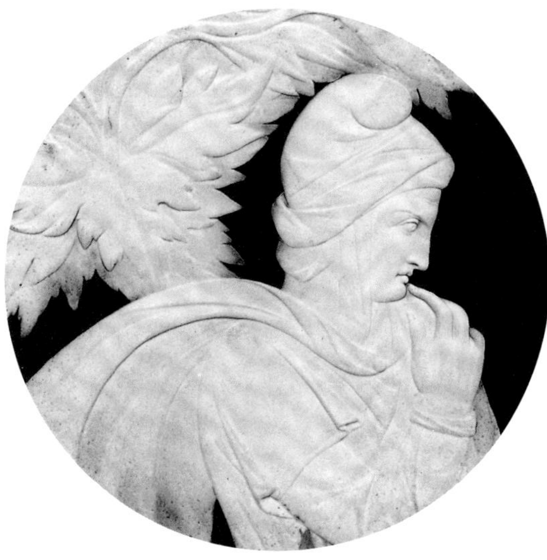

Detail of Wedgwood *Portland vase* (cat. no. 30), showing the base disc.

development of white stoneware, could take 'any tint of a fine blue, from the Lapis Lazuli to the lightest Onyx'.[21] Medallions in jasper were set like gems in all manner of small articles. They were intended for 'Rings, Buttons, Lockets and Bracelets; and especially for inlaying in fine Cabinets, Writing-Tables, Bookcases, &c'.[22]

It was not until 1779 that large plaques and vases were made in jasper. The plaques with light blue and green ground looked well with the pastel colours of the Neoclassical interior. They were designed to be set into large-scale decorative schemes in plaster, and were very successful as ornaments for mantelpieces.

A very important creamware service was also produced during the creative Wedgwood and Bentley partnership. This was the extensive table setting made for Catherine the Great of Russia and delivered in 1774 (see cat. no. 7). It required a great program of painting beyond the scope of the 'useful' creamwares of Josiah's Burslem partnership with Thomas Wedgwood.

WEDGWOOD IN THE LATE 18TH CENTURY

Wedgwood continued to expand his range of jasper wares after the death of Bentley in 1780, mastering the problems of making large plaques and vases, and collecting designs after the antique from artists working in Rome under the supervision of Flaxman, who was now an independent sculptor. At the Etruria factory artists also interpreted the designs of Lady Diana Beauclerc (see cat. no. 28) and Lady Templetown (see cat. no. 22). Their playful *putti* and figures of women and children engaged in domestic pursuits show a gentle and sentimental mood, and reflect the interest of the age in the virtues of a natural and unaffected life. Such subjects were ideally suited to smaller jasper vases and to the jasper teawares popular in the late 18th century.

However Wedgwood's proudest achievement in jasper was his success in reproducing the *Portland vase* (see cat. nos 30, 31). This famous example of ancient Roman cameo-glass was generously placed at the potter's disposal by the Duke of Portland. The ceramic version occupied Wedgwood's efforts for four years from 1787. Interestingly, the vase was produced in a subscribed edition, as if it were the publication of an important book. This was a new concept for ceramics,[23] and he wrote:

… it is evident, multiplying Copies of fine Works in durable Materials, must have the same Effect upon the *Arts* as the Invention of Printing has upon the *Sciences*; by these Means the principal Productions of both Kinds will be for ever preserved; and most effectually prevent the Return of ignorant and barbarous Ages.[24]

For Wedgwood as for other men of the 18th century, sometimes called 'the Age of Reason', there was an essential connection between the sciences, the arts and the trades (a view similarly expressed in the great French *Encyclopedie* of Denis Diderot, published between 1751 and 1772). Wedgwood believed not only in the importance of style but also in the mission of education.

As a scientist Wedgwood was a tireless experimenter in the cause of his ceramic art. He delivered several papers to the Royal Society and was awarded a fellowship of the Society for his invention of a pyrometer (the first of such instruments to measure high temperatures in the kiln). He was part of the scientific and philosophical circle of the Lunar Society, in which he could enjoy the company of artists and scientists alike.

The ideas and sentiments of the intellectual movement known as the Enlightenment were fostered in these circles and expressed with particular force in Wedgwood's *Slave medallion* of 1787 and the *Sydney Cove medallion* of 1789.[25] The earlier medallion was manufactured and distributed in support of the Society for the Suppression of the Slave Trade, of which Wedgwood was a member.[26] The 1789 medallion was an experiment using Sydney clay to determine the feasibility of setting up a pottery in the colony, or making other use of the natural resource. It shows, in exquisite Neoclassical relief, the figure of Hope addressing Peace, Labour and Art on the shores of Sydney Cove. As the *Slave medallion* reflects the humanitarian ideals of the Enlightenment, so the homage to the new settlement in Australia is a concise monument to the prevailing faith in progress through art and technology. Both works were praised for their 'new taste' and 'antient virtue'.[27]

Josiah Wedgwood died in 1795. As his monument in Stoke Parish church declares, he

converted the English pottery industry from 'a rude and inconsiderable Manufactory into an elegant Art and an important part of the National Commerce'.

WEDGWOOD IN THE 19TH CENTURY

Josiah Wedgwood had taken his three sons into partnership in 1790, and also his nephew Thomas Byerley (c.1747–1810). At his death, however, the partners in the firm were his son Josiah II Wedgwood (1769–1843) and Byerley, then in charge of the showrooms in Greek Street, Soho. The showrooms were soon moved to York House in St James's.

These were not prosperous times, but things improved when one of the sons, John Wedgwood (1766–1844), rejoined the firm in 1800, updated the factory's facilities and introduced new styles of ceramic. In 1801 the factory installed an up-to-the-minute steam engine to process the clay and to turn the potters' wheels.

At the end of 1805 Wedgwood began selling underglaze blue printed earthenwares, a cheaper line pioneered by Minton and others. Wares printed in blue and brown, and some with hand-coloured additions became popular. The range of ceramic bodies in production included caneware (see cat. nos 53–5), rosso antico (see cat. no. 49), pearlware (a whiter version of creamware), stone china (a durable, highly vitrified body, see cat. no. 61) and others, along with the jasper and basalt. From 1812 until the sale of their London showroom in 1829, Wedgwood made a brief foray into the production of bone china (see cat. no. 58). This was the now classic English porcelain body pioneered by the firms of Spode and Minton, made with a substantial addition of burnt bone to a mixture of china clay, china stone and flint. Its manufacture was not resumed by Wedgwood until 1878; today it is a staple product.

After John Wedgwood's death there seems to have been a further decline under a series of less interested family members. The factory was partly sold up in 1843, when Francis Wedgwood was in partnership with John Boyle, formerly of Minton & Boyle. But things began to look up under the subsequent partnership (1846–59) of Francis Wedgwood and Robert Brown when industrial techniques were further upgraded. In 1846 Wedgwood showed with the Society of

Arts, Manufactures and Commerce (later the Royal Society of Arts) in London, at its third annual exhibition.[28]

The Great Exhibition of 1851 at the Crystal Palace, London, intended to show the 'Works of Industry of All Nations', was a focus of the most florid phase of Victorian design. Wedgwood's exhibit, however, was among the more restrained and showed the continuing importance of the jasper wares for the firm's reputation. According to the *Art Journal* catalogue:

> The entire series of works displayed by the present firm are of the classic form and style of decoration, so well known to connoisseurs; the ground of each article being of a lavender tint … There is much simplicity in the general character of the floral and other ornament … and we rejoice to see this eminent house again prepared to assert its position among the principal Art-manufactures of the present day; attesting to the deserved character obtained for the establishment by the famous Josiah Wedgwood.

The catalogue also acknowledged some statues which were in the new 'Carrara' matt-surfaced porcelain body developed by Wedgwood to parallel the 'Parian' of Minton. The material was used to popularise classical and modern sculpture. The fuller catalogue of 'class 25' of the 1851 exhibition lists a wide variety of types: terracotta with black reliefs; creamware, including 18th-century designs; goods for the laboratory and the bathroom; etc.

The high prestige of the older designs was underlined by special exhibitions of early Wedgwood at the *Manchester Art Treasures* exhibition in 1857 and at the South Kensington (now the Victoria and Albert) Museum in 1862.

In the late 1850s the French-trained artist Emile Lessore (1805–76) introduced a new approach to painting on earthenware (see cat. no. 65), working at Etruria until 1863 and continuing to paint for Wedgwood after returning to France that year. His simplicity and informality were especially prized by Godfrey Wedgwood, and a critic writing in the *Art Journal* catalogue of the 1862 exhibition praised Lessore's work as 'very bold and free in treatment, highly effective, and

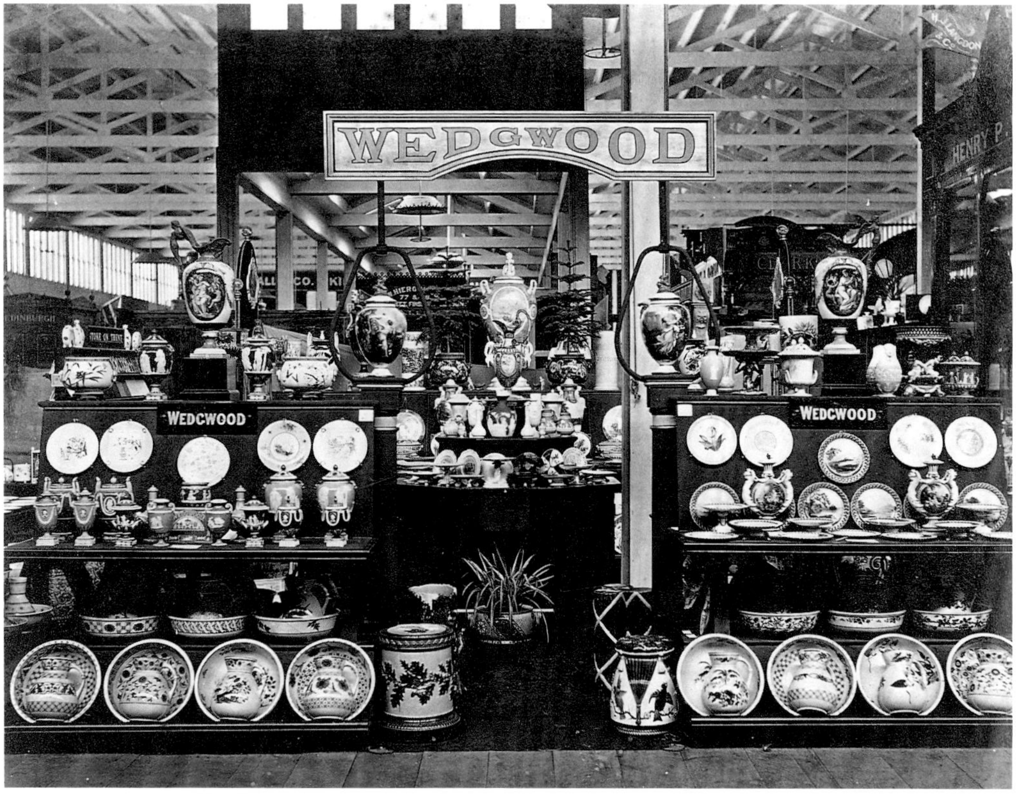

Photograph of the Wedgwood stand at the Melbourne International Exhibition 1880–81.
Photo courtesy of the National Trust.

veritable examples of pure Art — PICTURES, painted by a true ARTIST on the material of the POTTER'.

It was not until the 1860s that Wedgwood started making 'majolica', a type of pottery with bright transparent glazes which had brought success to the Minton factory in 1851,[29] and named after the colourful pottery made in Italy and France in the period of the Renaissance. The technique was soon adapted to the taste of the Aesthetic movement, incorporating influences from Japanese design (see cat. no. 69).

In a more radical vein was the work of the designer Christopher Dresser (1834–1904), not so averse to the machine as his contemporaries in the Arts and Crafts movement. Dresser provided designs for Wedgwood (about1865–80), while also working with Minton. His extant designs include a boldly geometric cylinder vase with angular, abstract decoration anticipating the Art Deco style, and an exotic Egyptian-style border design named after the goddess Isis.

In the 1870s Wedgwood was joined by the designers Charles Toft (1832–1909) (see cat. no. 67) and Thomas Allen (1831–1915) who came in 1876, later became art director and stayed until 1905. Both men had matured their skills at Minton's, but relished the relative freedom to design which the Wedgwood establishment gave to its artists. Their work could be seen at the Paris Exhibition of 1878, alongside *pâte-sur-pâte* decoration[30] by another former Minton employee Frederick Rhead (1857–1933).

In 1878 the company again acquired a London showroom (first at Holborn Circus, then after 1890 at Hatton Gardens), and the reintroduction of bone china in the same year inaugurated an important aspect of mass manufacture. The later 19th century seems to have seen little interesting stylistic development,[31] but it was a period of considerable activity in promoting Wedgwood wares at international exhibitions, including in Melbourne and Sydney (see cat. nos 69, 71, 72).

WEDGWOOD IN THE 20TH CENTURY

In 1903 Alfred Powell (1865–1960) began his association with Wedgwood (see cat. no. 73). Trained as an architect, he made an important contribution through the decorating studio he set up for Wedgwood in Bloomsbury with his wife Louise (1882–1956), grand-daughter of Emile Lessore. The Powells' work came out of the Arts and Crafts movement inspired by John Ruskin and William Morris, and many of Powell's designers were trained, like Louise, at the Central School of Arts and Crafts where the influential architect–designer and critic W.R. Lethaby was co-principal. These designers were concerned to cleanse the crafts of ornamentation, which had become debased through mechanical repetition, and return to simplicity and quality which they associated with intelligence and honesty as well as beauty. Powell's designs were also adapted at Etruria. In the 1920s, there was a small handcraft school at Etruria, under Millicent Taplin (1902–80), which continued the Arts and Crafts philosophy.

John Goodwin (1867–1949) was the Wedgwood factory's art director from 1904 where, apart from his interest in the Powells, he generally fostered a conservative production. However, stylish tablewares were designed just before 1914 by French designers Paul Follet and Marcel Goupy. Intended for the French market, these wares were not produced until the 1920s because of the First World War. They have a clean, classic quality with a hint of the Art Deco exhibition of Paris 1925, with decoration in the form of stripes and simple florals. In very different taste were the lushly decorative 'Fairyland lustre' wares of Daisy Makeig-Jones (1881–1945), which were made at Etruria from 1915 to 1931 and achieved popular acclaim for their story-book decoration in exotic colours reminiscent of the Russian ballet of Diaghelev.

On Goodwin's retirement in 1934 he was replaced as art director by Victor Skellern (1909–66). Skellern was heir to Goodwin's encouragement of the architect Keith Murray (1892–1981) whose severe forms, first shown in 1933, were decorated with mostly monochrome glazes and represent Wedgwood's most radical excursion into Modernism. The highly stylised but essentially decorative animal designs of sculptor John Skeaping (1901–80) were, meanwhile, the leading expression of Wedgwood's Art Deco sculptural style. Skellern's best decorative work is based on the attractive contemporary style of British wood-engraving. He favoured utilitarian and harmonious designs, presiding over the period when Wedgwood was associated with the Council for Art and Industry and the Dorland Hall Exhibition of 1933, and also an important exhibition at Grafton Galleries in 1936. In this exhibition Norman Wilson (b. 1902), the leading technician of the period, showed coloured bodies and new glazes, including fine effects influenced by Chinese ceramics, which unfortunately could not be put into commercial production. Skellern formed Wedgwood's link with the designer,

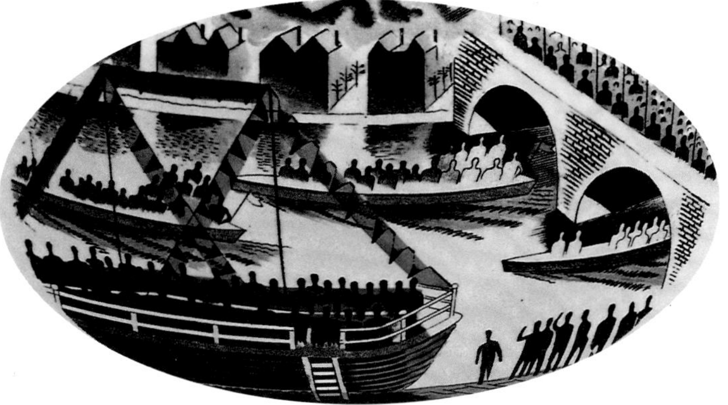

Detail of Wedgwood *Boat Race bowl* designed by Eric Ravilious (see cat. no. 74).

watercolourist and graphic artist Eric Ravilious (1903–42) who made some excellent designs for the company between 1936 and 1940 (see cat. no. 74).

At the end of the 1930s the factory began its move several miles to the south, to new buildings designed by Keith Murray at Barlaston. Progress was impeded by the Second World War, but in the 1940s Arnold Machin made some amiable figurines which combine humour, abstraction and a sober appreciation of the problems of production without skilled workers (see cat. no. 76).

Wedgwood has continued to bring in leading artists in recent decades. Teaware designs commissioned in 1960 from the important Austrian-trained British studio potter Lucie Rie (b. 1902) were not thought suitable for production, but in 1971 Wedgwood commissioned British sculptor and printmaker Eduardo Paolozzi to design a set of six plates in a limited edition. These were in British Pop Art style, strongly influenced by machine forms.

Wedgwood has also fostered studio ceramics through work with Glenys Barton in 1976–77 (see cat. nos 77, 78) and in 1982 the major British jeweller Wendy Ramshaw designed for Wedgwood, combining ceramic elements in jasper ware with precious metal.

The company, which already exported to the New World, Russia and Turkey in the 18th century, continues to be appreciated widely for its tablewares, and for the famous blue jasper derived from its Neoclassical past.

Notes

1 Dr Robert Plot, first Keeper of the Ashmolean Museum at Oxford, published remarks on the potteries in his topographical survey, *Natural History of Staffordshire,* in 1686.
2 Originally the lead ore was dusted onto creamware before firing, a method which led rapidly to lead-poisoning. Later, it was applied in liquid form to the fired but unglazed (biscuit) ware. Salt glaze is achieved by throwing common salt (sodium chloride) into the kiln. It volatilises and the sodium combines with the clay to form a glossy surface.
3 The white clay was of the pipe-clay type, also called ball-clay from the form in which is was brought in.
4 The flint stones were 'calcined', that is, they were heated and crushed, using windmill power, to provide the silica content otherwise supplied by local sands.
5 Japanese porcelain was hard to obtain by mid century. Imported European porcelain was only for the wealthy few, and the earliest English porcelain of Chelsea (from 1745), and then Bow, Derby and Worcester, still supplied only a luxury market.
6 Josiah Spode (d. 1797) was a successful potter and father of Josiah II Spode who turned his business into one which outstripped Wedgwood in the early 19th century. William Greatbatch (1735–1813) also became an important potter in his own right. See Barker (1991).
7 see Reilly (1989) vol. I, p. 29.
8 see Barker (1991).
9 see Reilly (1989) vol. I, p. 165.
10 Traditionally the craftsman's career was divided into time spent as apprentice, journeyman and master. The journeyman, a qualified artisan following his apprenticeship, would travel about, learning from various masters while working for wages.
11 This was an extensive tea and coffee service for twelve, and included twelve candlesticks. It would have been moulded with flowers and glazed green, the gilding of the background being applied over the glaze. See Finer & Savage (1965) p. 34.
12 Finer & Savage (1965) p. 55.
13 Dating from the 6th to the 4th centuries BC, they were, in fact, generally imports from Greece or from the Greek colonies of southern Italy.
14 Sir John Soane, architect, whose remarkable house and collection of antiquities now forms the Soane Museum in London. He was a major architect of the generation after Adam.
15 Books included d'Hancarville's volumes of Sir William Hamilton's vases published 1766–67 (see cat. no. 11), James 'Athenian' Stuart's work on

Greek architecture published in 1766, and the vast compilations of antiquities by the Comte de Caylus and others. Wedgwood would also have been able to see books of this type in private or public libraries, and seems to have been familiar with the illustrations of Montfaucon (see cat. nos 30, 62). See also Macht (1957).

16 Wedgwood to Bentley 1771: 'Mr Freeman says he knows young Flaxman is a Coxcomb but does not think him a bit the worse for it, or less likely to be a great artist'. (Kelly (1965) p. 58)

17 Wedgwood's black basalt was a black stoneware developed by Josiah I in 1768 from a local black earthenware called 'Egyptian black'. It was coloured with iron (from ochre) and with manganese, and fired to a glossy surface.

18 Wedgwood & Bentley, *A Catalogue*, 1779, p. 23.

19 Wedgwood's jasper was a unique stoneware body, rich in barium sulphate (barytes) and barium carbonate (witherite), these minerals being mined in Derbyshire. See Reilly (1989) vol. I, pp. 521–38. It was either coloured throughout (e.g. with cobalt blue) or enhanced with an applied slip of coloured jasper (jasper dip). Parts in relief were made separately in plaster moulds, from a design typically executed in wax. The white relief decoration was then attached to the coloured ground before firing. (Less often the ground was white and/or the reliefs were in coloured jasper.)

20 Kelly (1965) pp. 62–3. The relief had recently been acquired from the Borghese collection in Rome.

21 Finer & Savage (1965) p. 170.

22 Wedgwood & Bentley, *A Catalogue*, 1779, p. 2.

23 In a somewhat similar fashion, in the 19th century, ceramic replicas of sculpture made by Minton and Copeland were offered as prizes by the Art Union.

24 Wedgwood & Bentley, *A Catalogue*, 1779, pp. 48–9.

25 Richard L. Smith (1978).

26 Benjamin Franklin was among those to whom he personally sent examples.

27 In Erasmus Darwin's poem *The Botanic Garden*, where he sees 'fair HOPE' attempting to 'cheer the dreary wastes of Sydney-Cove' (Part I, Canto II, lines 313 ff.). Wedgwood's friend Darwin, physician and 'natural philosopher', was the grandfather of the scientist Charles Darwin who postulated the theory of evolution.

28 Works included a dolphin salt-cellar designed by the sculptor John Bell, and marked with the initials of Felix Summerly (pseudonym of design reformer Henry Cole) who promoted the cause of the Great Exhibition of 1851 and was the first director of the South Kensington (later Victoria and Albert) Museum.

29 Wedgwood's green-glazed dessert wares and lead-glazed brown Rockingham wares, already in production at the time, supplied a similar market niche in respect of tablewares.

30 This technique, of which Louis-Marc Solon at Minton was the master, consisted of building up designs in white slip on a coloured ground, the Parian-type body fusing to transparency in the thinner parts of the design.

31 There were technical innovations however, including 'Victoria ware', a highly coloured and gilt type using either a creamware or Parian-type body, and a type of basalt very richly bronzed and gilded.

CATALOGUE

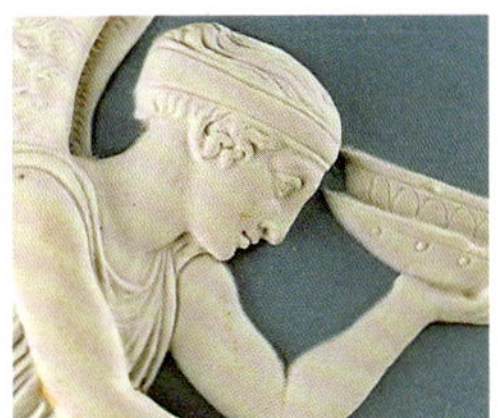

1 *Cauliflower jug* 1759-65

earthenware (creamware)
14.2 x 8.9 x 7.7 cm
Unmarked
K. and N. Deutsher collection

The lidded jug is moulded to resemble a cauliflower and decorated with green glaze on cream. It is of a type which appears among the first pottery made by Josiah I Wedgwood, and exemplifies the amusing, naturalistic forms favoured by the playful spirit of the Rococo.[1] Similar pieces were made by several potters of the period, including Thomas Whieldon (1719–95) and William Greatbatch (1735–1813). Josiah Wedgwood was an indefatigable experimental chemist from early in his career. His experiment book[2] has been preserved and shows that on 23 March 1759 he developed an improved green glaze for such pieces, when he was still working with Whieldon. Greatbatch seems to have

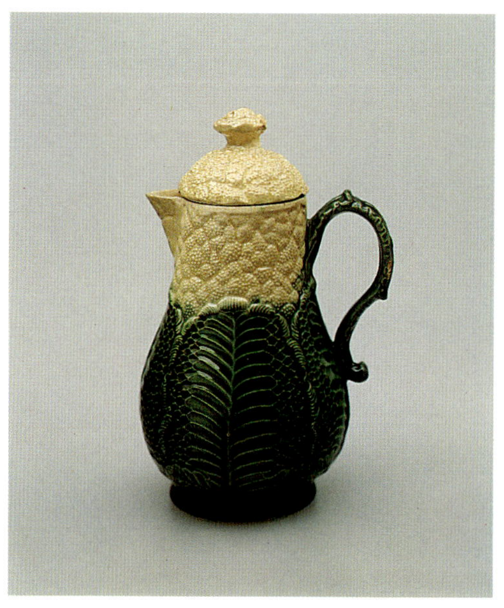

supplied Wedgwood with consignments of moulded wares, presumably as a supplement to his own production.

NOTES

1   Reilly (1989) vol. I, pl. C13, illustrates a jug in the Zeitlin collection, moulded from an apparently identical block but with a different handle, and attributed to Wedgwood, about 1763. For a contemporary reference to Wedgwood's 'Colly flower ware' see Reilly (1989) vol. I, p. 165.

2   This is preserved in a manuscript copy of about 1782 in the Wedgwood Museum, Barlaston.

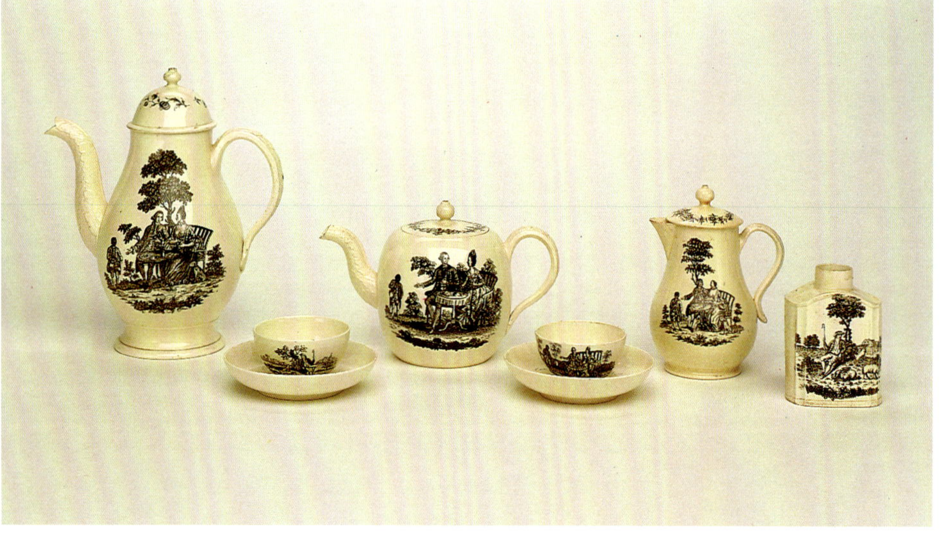

2 *Group of tea and coffee wares* 1764–70

earthenware (creamware)
coffee pot 24.1 x 21.1 x 13.0 cm
Impressed mark: [WEDG]WOOD
Incised mark: ⟶
teapot 13.3 x 20.8 x 12.0 cm
Impressed mark: WEDGW[O]OD
Incised triangle and circle
jug 15.6 x 11.4 x 9.0 cm
tea caddy 10.6 x 7.6 x 5.2 cm
teabowl 4.2 x 7.8 x 7.8 cm
Incised triangle
saucer 12.2 x 12.2 x 2.8 cm
Incised circle
Presented through The Art Foundation of Victoria by Mr Keith M. Deutsher, Founder Benefactor 1993   (D9-1993)

The teapot and coffee pot with cabbage-moulded spouts and overlapping leaf handles, the lidded milk jug, a tea caddy, two teabowls and saucers are decorated with the 'Tea party' and 'Shepherd' patterns transfer-printed in brownish black by Sadler & Green.[1] Wedgwood sent glazed ware to be decorated by this Liverpool firm from 1761 to 1795. The designs were etched on copper plates and retouched with engraving tools. They were then printed in oil on a flexible 'bat' or 'paper'[2] of glue, transferred to the glazed ware and dusted with colour to be fired. The prints show a number of variations. Designs were produced in

different sizes to fit various pieces and worn printing plates needed to be replaced.

Sadler & Green was among the first to use transfer printing on ceramics, a technique which Sadler claimed to have invented for himself, around 1750. By the mid-1750s transfer printing was also in use (independently) at the Bow and Worcester porcelain factories, and for enamel snuff boxes. In the efficient form developed by Sadler & Green it enabled complex designs to be created quickly and cheaply for the first time in the history of ceramics.

NOTES

1   John Sadler (1720–89) and Guy Green (active 1750–99). The earliest record of their business with Wedgwood dates from 23 September 1761. See Roberts (1986) especially for technical information of the firm's printing methods; also Reilly & Savage (1980) p. 335. Sadler retired in 1770 and Green continued the business.

2   Holdway (1990).

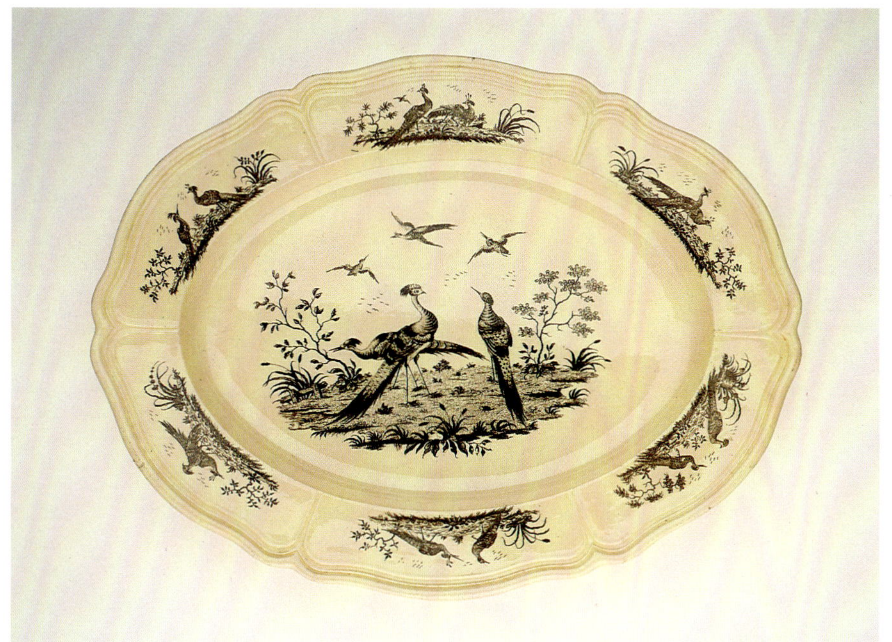

3 *Dish* c. 1770

earthenware (creamware)
27.8 x 35.9 x 3.0 cm
Impressed mark: WEDGWOOD
K. and N. Deutsher collection

The oval dish is made in the 'Queen's shape' with a simple lobed border of a type often found in silver. It is overglaze printed in black with exotic birds in a landscape, a type of decoration found in colours on porcelain of the day, especially at Worcester but also at Longton Hall, Liverpool and elsewhere. On Wedgwood it is known as 'Liver birds' (the birds which support the arms of the city of Liverpool). The transfer print was executed by Sadler & Green (see cat. no. 2).

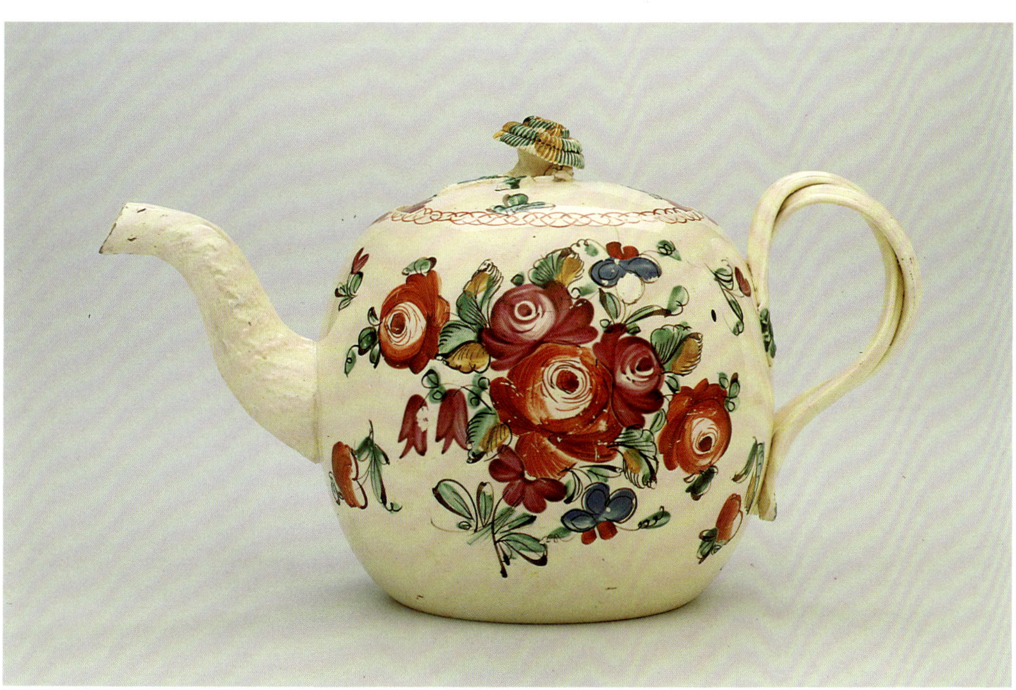

4 *Teapot* c. 1770

earthenware (creamware)
14.8 x 25.3 x 14.0 cm
Impressed mark: Wedgwood
Incised: ∿
Presented through The Art Foundation of Victoria by Mrs Norma Deutsher, Governor 1994   (D20-1994)

The globular teapot has a cabbage-moulded spout and a double handle formed by two reeded straps crossed over each other and terminating in leaves. The lid has a finial in the form of a flower with sharply striated petals, similar to a type used on Leeds creamware, but supported by a pad of clay in a manner typical of Wedgwood. It is relatively rare to find a marked example of this type of teapot.[1]

The teapot is painted in brightly coloured enamels with floral sprays including roses, in the manner of the David Rhodes workshop. Wedgwood's association with David Rhodes began at Leeds around 1764, and from 1768 Rhodes was decorating Wedgwood in London. From about 1770 he was manager of Wedgwood's own decorating studio in Cheyne Row, Chelsea. He died in 1777.

NOTE

1   The mark, which would have been made with separate letters, has some odd defects but is comparable with the accepted mark in Rakow & Rakow (1981) fig. 26B.

5 *Husk pattern plate* c. 1770

earthenware (creamware)
25.0 x 24.8 x 2.2 cm
Impressed mark: WEDGWOOD
K. and N. Deutsher collection

5a *Husk pattern plate* c. 1810
Poskotchin factory, Morye, Russia

earthenware (creamware)
24.9 x 24.8 x 2.3 cm
Mark: C.▯
K. and N. Deutsher collection

The Wedgwood creamware plate is made in the 'Queen's shape'. The rim is decorated in purplish pink with a pendant garland of husks. In the centre is a flower and leaf motif. An extensive service of this pattern was delivered to the Empress Catherine II of Russia in 1774, and survives in the palace of Petrodvorets (Peterhof). Some pieces were sold by permission of the state this century.

Replacements for the service, made about 1810 at the Poskotchin Factory near St Petersburg, indicate that the service stayed in use. The pieces make an interesting comparison: the Russian potting is very fine, but the decoration is

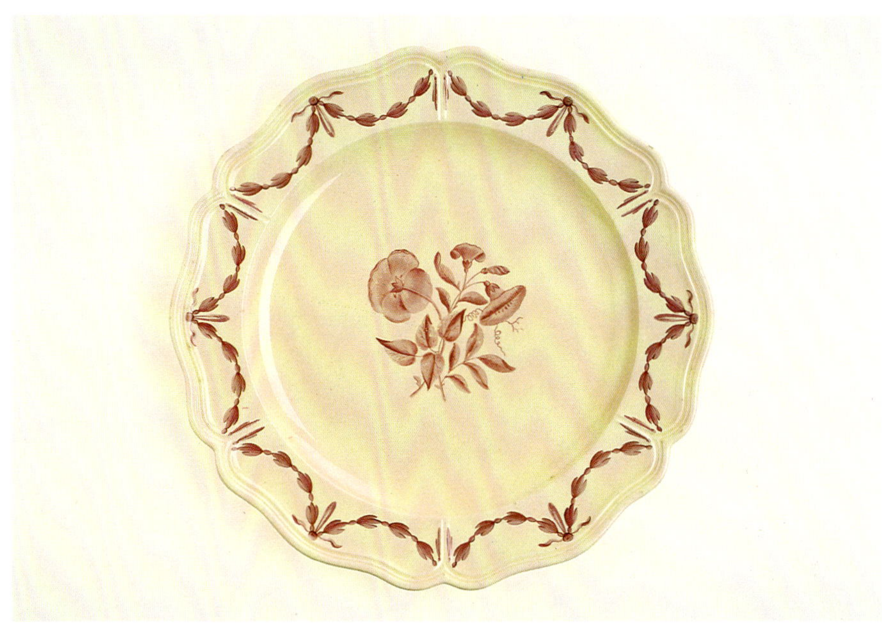

more schematic than Wedgwood's, and darker in colour.

Wedgwood exported widely in the 18th century and sherds from a similar Wedgwood 'Husk' pattern service have been excavated at Colonial Williamsburg in the United States.

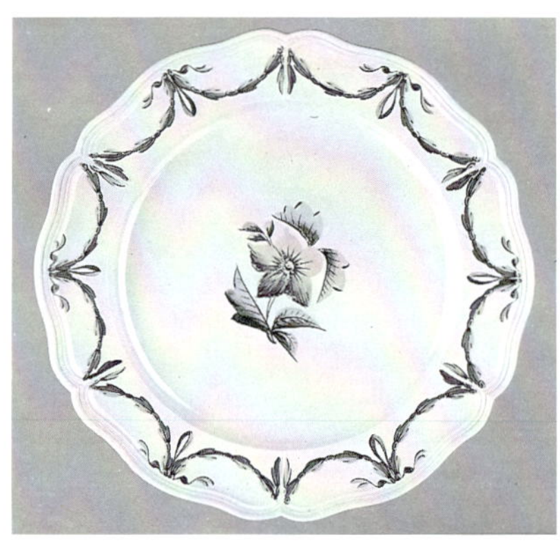

6 *Plate* 1770–90

earthenware (creamware)
25.3 x 25.3 x 2.3 cm
Impressed mark: WEDGWOOD
Incised mark in the form of the outline of a shield
Presented through The Art Foundation of Victoria by Mr Keith M. Deutsher, Founder Benefactor 1993   (D10-1993)

The dinner plate is painted in blue enamel with an 'antique dart' border containing an armorial crest. In the centre is a floral spray. The radical simplicity of creamwares ornamented with Wedgwood's new border patterns was an ideal foil for armorial decoration. Wedgwood often used printing for armorials (see Drakard (1986)) and although it is not evident on the present example the neatness and symmetry suggest the painter could have used a printed guide which was allowed to burn away.

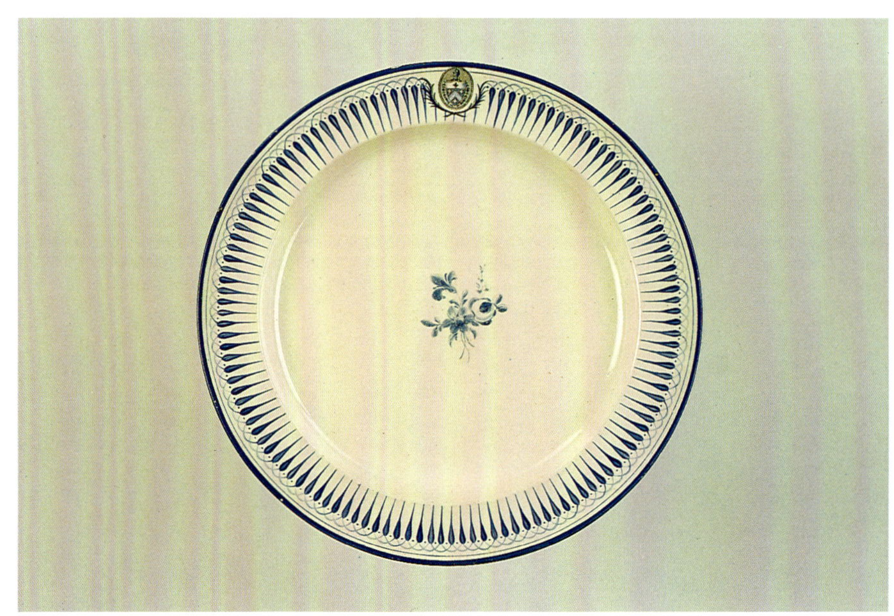

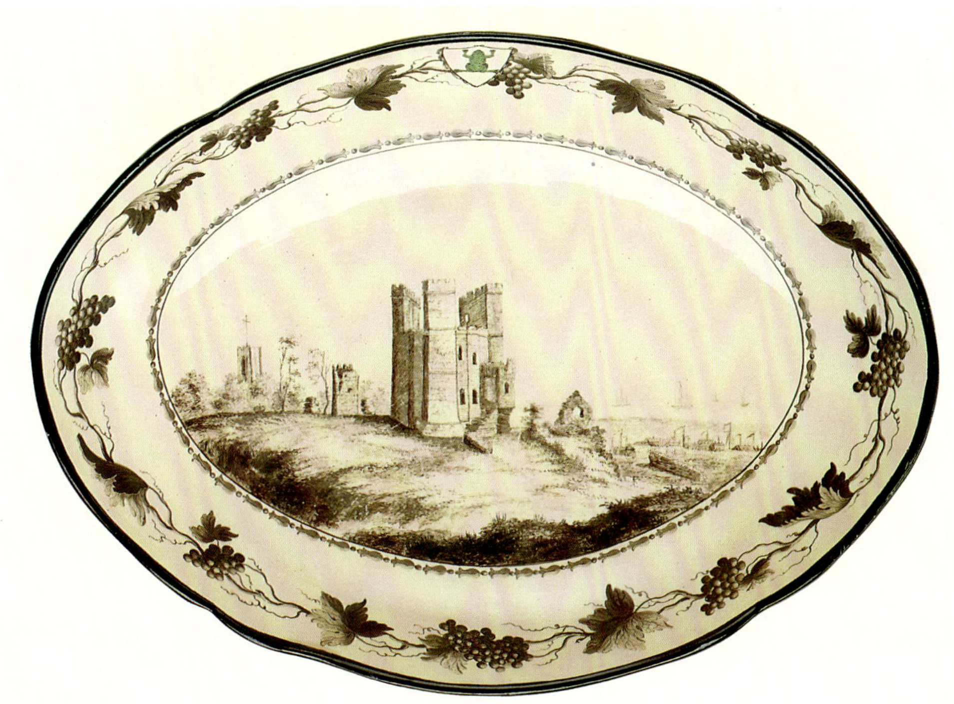

7 *Dessert dish, possibly a trial piece for the* Frog service *c. 1773*

earthenware (creamware)
21.5 x 29.2 x 5.4 cm
Impressed mark: WEDGWOOD
Presented through The Art Foundation of
Victoria by Mr Keith M. Deutsher, Founder
Benefactor 1993   (D7-1993)

The oval dish is decorated in blackish brown with a view of a crenellated castle set among ruins, and a seaport in the distance. The landscape is set within a narrow husk border. The outer grapevine border bears a shield with a frog emblem in green.

Preserved in the Hermitage Museum, St Petersburg, is the famous *Frog Service*[1] made about 1773 for the Empress Catherine of Russia. This extensive service was ordered for the Empress's country retreat called 'La Grenouillère' ('The Frogmarsh') and, like the present dish, bears a crest in the form of a green frog. It was produced by the Wedgwood and Bentley partnership, although table wares were normally made by Josiah Wedgwood in partnership with his cousin Thomas Wedgwood. The great service of 952 pieces entailed some 1244 views of British country houses and gardens, landscapes and picturesque ruins. It was ordered through the Russian

Consul in London, Alexander Baxter. Painting began in the spring of 1773, and was executed in Wedgwood's decorating studio at Chelsea.

The Russian service was executed in monochrome (except for the green frog). The dinner service has oak borders and a decorated fluted border within, while the dessert has an ivy border and an inner border of 'Etruscan' *ovolo* design. A number of coloured pieces, without the frog emblem, were painted shortly after the completion of the Russian order. They were until recently thought to be trial pieces, made before the decision had been taken to paint the service in less costly monochrome. The present dish is quite different from these and may indeed be a trial, undertaken before the design was finalised,[2] or possibly to try out the skills of new painters.

The scene is the west view of Orford Castle, Suffolk, after S.& N. Buck, *The Antiquities of England and Wales*, London, 1744, vol. II. A circular plate, no 868 in the Russian service as delivered in 1775, depicts the same view.[3]

The mediaeval castle complies with the Empress's initial request, which was for views of buildings in the Gothic style, to complement her new palace at La Grenouillère (properly called the Chesme palace).[4] This was in the form of a triangular mediaeval castle with towers, and one of the earliest examples of

Gothic Revival style in Russia. The English provided the lead in this style, as in garden design and the new appreciation of wild scenery, aspects of 18th-century taste which were also reflected in the subjects executed for the *Frog Service*.

The service was put on display in Wedgwood's London showrooms in June 1774, to be inspected by Queen Charlotte, and admired by the world of fashion. Public entry was by ticket. A selection of the Russian pieces was again put on display by Wedgwood in London in 1909.

NOTES

1   Dukelskaya (1979) pl. 279-87; Haydon (1986); Kelly (1980); Reilly (1989) vol. I, pp. 271–82; Raeburn (1990).
2   Deutsher (1984). The present dish bears an old paper label: 'OXFORD ST. / MORTLOCKS / LONDON'. It was more recently exhibited in the Josiah Wedgwood Jubilee Exhibition 1980 at the First Bank of the U.S., organised by the Wedgwood International Seminar.
3   Information on the views and their sources has been supplied by Michael Raeburn, by personal communication to K. Deutsher.
4   Haydon (1986).

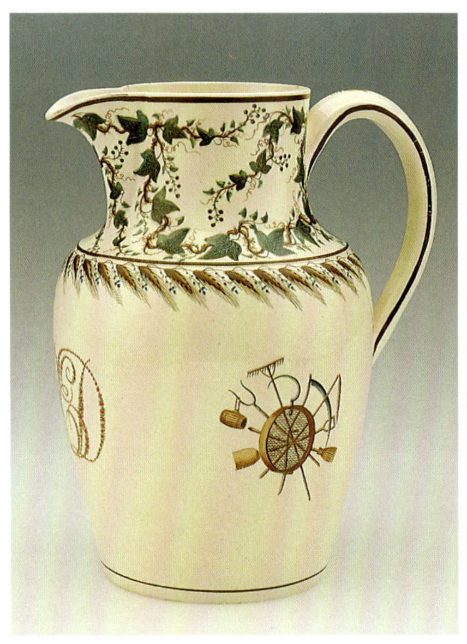

8 *Jug* c. 1795

earthenware (creamware)
23.0 x 19.8 x 15.3 cm
Impressed mark: WEDGWOOD / > >
Monogram below spout: RED
Presented by John H. Connell 1914   (1174-2)

This type of jug was produced to celebrate the harvest, and its body is decorated with trophies of agricultural implements, one side including a sheaf of wheat and a plough, the other a winnowing sieve, scythe, rake and other hand tools, together with a small water barrel for the thirsty harvester. The upper section has trails of green ivy and a brown line edge, while the shoulder has a formal border of ears of wheat. The owner's initials beneath the spout have been spelt out with red roses.

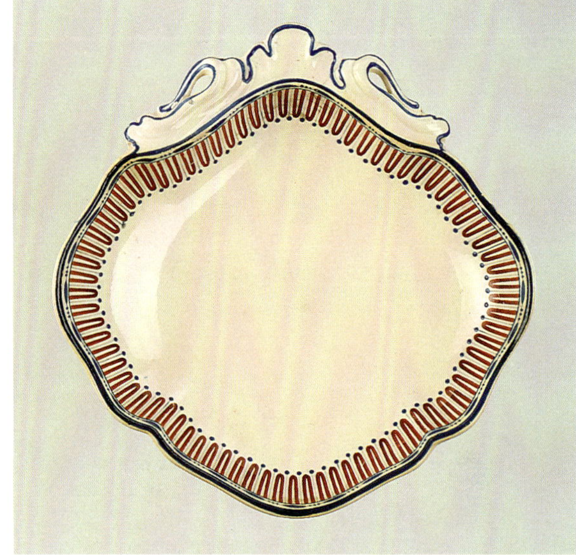

9 *Dessert Dish* 1770–90

earthenware (creamware)
21.9 x 21.2 x 4.6 cm
Impressed mark: WEDGWOOD / P
Presented through The Art Foundation of Victoria by Mr Keith M. Deutsher, Founder Benefactor 1993   (D11-1993)

The scalloped diamond-shaped dish is moulded with a scroll handle and decorated with an 'Etruscan' border in iron-red enamel with a husk garland and a line at the edge in dark blue.

10 *Cream vase* c. 1790

earthenware (creamware)
37.4 x 33.4 x 26.8 cm
Painted in brown on body and on lid: SL
Impressed mark: WEDGWOOD
Presented through The Art Foundation of Victoria by Mrs Norman Deutsher, Governor 1994   (D24-1994)

The shield-shaped vessel has horizontal handles in the manner of a Greek vase, and a lid which rises in an ogee curve towards a broad vent at the top. Both pieces are decorated with a band of 'flute and wreath' design in brown and blue (also known as 'lag and feather' pattern), crisply painted with just a hint of illusionistic depth. The initials 'SL' and simple brown line borders complete the decoration.

This dairy vase in the severe but elegant Neoclassical style was created in response to the 18th-century fashion for ladies to entertain guests with a visit to the dairy of their country house, where refreshments would be offered as part of a tour of the garden. There are over twenty 18th-century orders in the Wedgwood archives for tiles and dairy equipment. For example, Lady Spencer, returning from France where Marie-Antoinette's second dairy[1] was just being built, ordered a complete suite of matching tiles, cream vases etc. from Wedgwood in 1786. That ensemble, with simple ivy wreaths on creamware, survives at Althorp.[2] Marie-Antoinette's dairy was to be furnished with French porcelain cups of 'Etruscan' shape developed 1787–88 at the royal factory at Sèvres, while the Duc d'Orleans ordered Wedgwood for his dairy at le Raincy in 1788.

The Greek-style handles of the present vase,[3] which differ from the Althorp examples, suggest its designer had already seen the remarkable 'Etruscan' dessert service of Greek shapes, made at the Royal Factory of Naples and sent to George III by Ferdinand IV in 1788. Certainly Wedgwood produced a similar 'Etruscan' service shortly afterwards. The diplomatic gift had been on display in London.[4]

NOTES

1   Her first dairy was at the Petit Trianon, at Versailles. The furnishings do not survive. For the second dairy, at Rambouillet, see Schwarz (1992).
2   The stone building had a thatched roof in cottage style, and was possibly designed by Henry Holland, who was working at Althorp at this time. Dairies could be built in an amazing variety of styles: Holland designed a dairy in chinoiserie style at Woburn, built in the 1790s, and Wedgwood furnished one in an equally arbitrary Egyptian style about 1802.
3   A similar shape was supplied to the Duke of Bedford about 1820, see Reilly (1989) vol, II, fig. 9.
4   It was decorated with paintings of vases excavated at Naples. See Tait (1986).

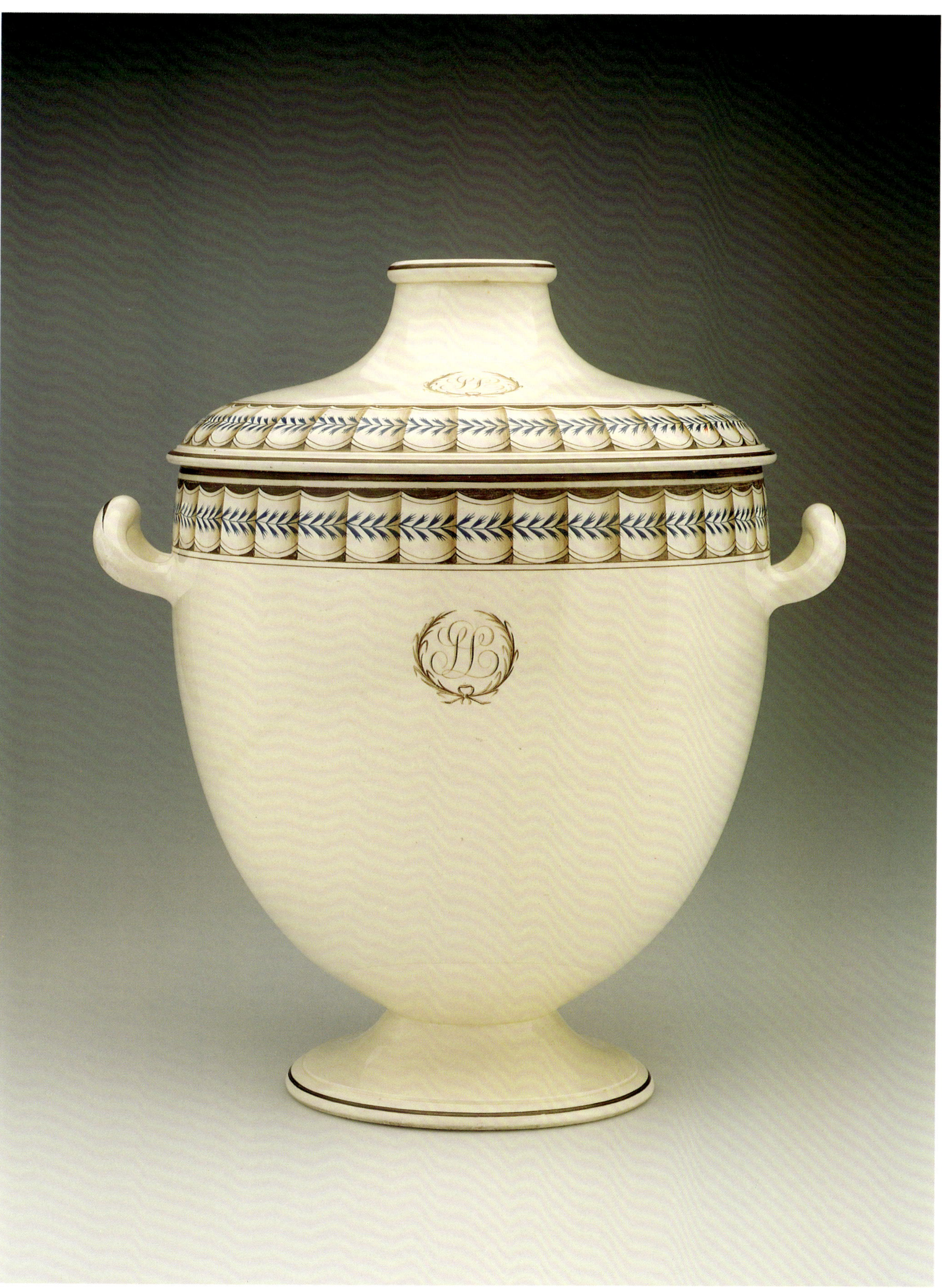

11 *Vase and cover* 1769–80

stoneware (basalt)
27.0 x 13.5 x 13.9 cm
Impressed circular mark on plinth:
WEDGWOOD & BENTLEY: ETRURIA.
K. and N. Deutsher collection

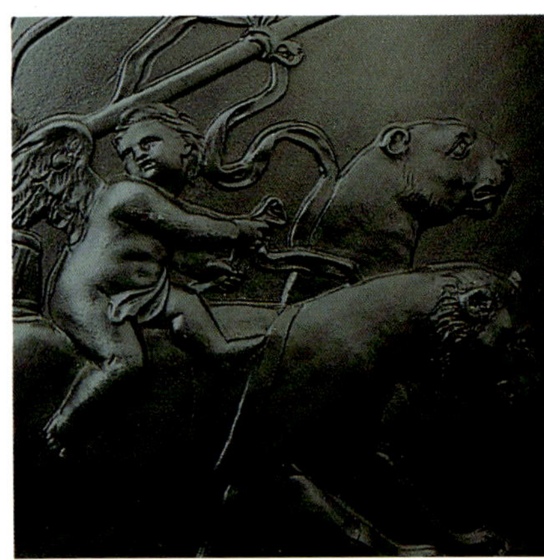

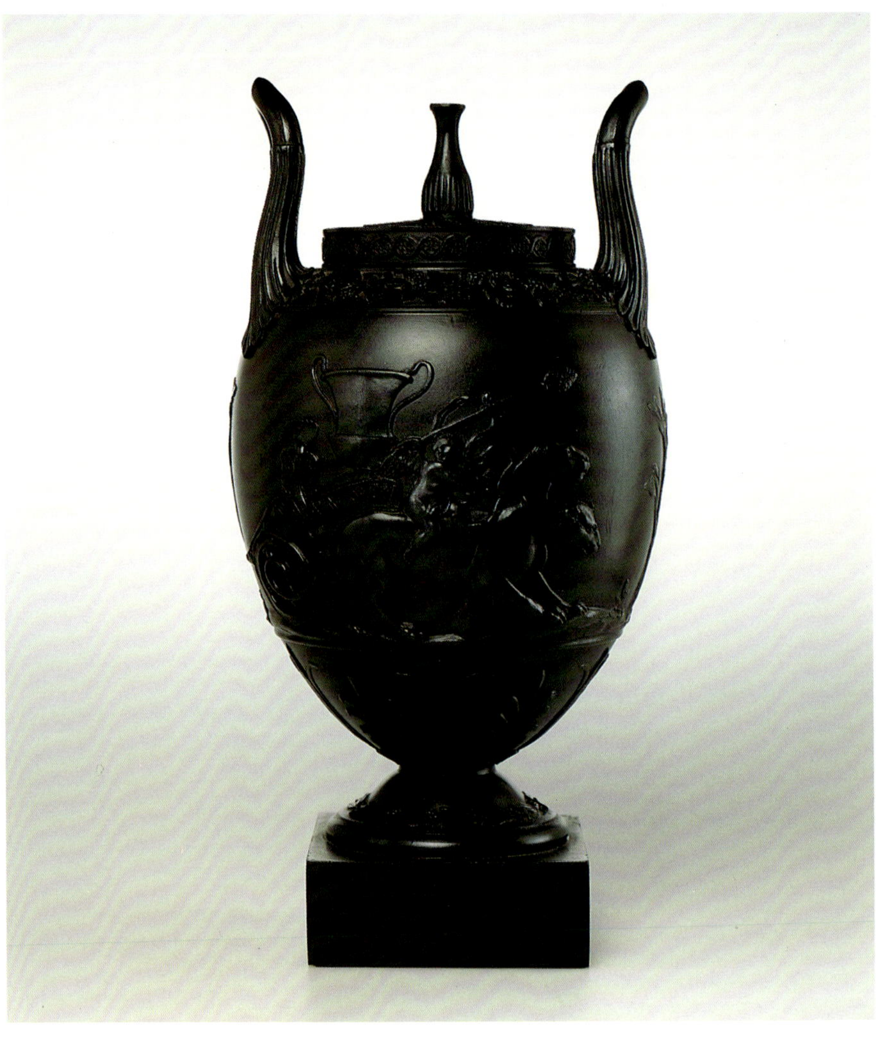

The vase has upright loop handles and a
flat lid with a baluster-shaped finial. It is
decorated in relief with a chariot drawn
by two panthers and carrying a boy with
trophies appropriate for Bacchus, the
reverse with a chariot drawn by rams and
carrying two winged boys and trophies
proper to Mercury (a design known in
Wedgwood as 'Cupid and the infant
Mercury').

This design derives from a Roman
sarcophagus now in the Capitoline
Museum.[1] The shape of this vase was
inspired by an ancient Greek type, the
lebes gamikos. Only recently Sir William
Hamilton's collection of ancient vases had
been published in four volumes, with
luxurious and unusually accurate
illustrations (d'Hancarville 1766–7). The
work includes at least two vases of a
shape comparable to the present one
(vol. II, pl. 36 and vol. III, pl.109).

As early as 1768 Lord Cathcart
apparently gave Wedgwood access to this
influential work, whose express intent
was to raise the taste of the artists of the
age, as well as to inform the antiquarian.
D'Hancarville announced he would give
greater attention to proportion in the
study of ceramics than earlier authors,
and went on to say:

> We should think we had not
> advanced one step forwarder if the
> Monuments we publish were to the
> Artists merely the objects of fruitless
> admiration, but shall think we have
> gone something farther if it should

prove that we revive an ancient art
… In every Art good models give
birth to ideas, by exciting the
imagination, theory furnishes the
means of expressing those ideas,
practice puts these means in
execution and this last part, which is
always the most common, is also the
easiest. (vol. I, p. viii)

> We think also, that we make an
> agreeable present to our
> Manufacturers of earthern ware and
> China, glass, marble &c. Having
> employed much more time in
> working than in reflexion, being
> besides in great want of models, they
> will be very glad to find here more
> than two hundred forms, the greatest
> part of which, are absolutely new to
> them … (vol. I, p. xviii)

Wedgwood may not have been so
dismissive of the practical part of art but
his technical innovation would surely
have not achieved the same success

without the radical rethinking of style
encouraged by contemporary
antiquarians (and the progressive
architects of the day).

Wedgwood and Bentley commenced
work at their new factory, Etruria, in
1769. It was named after that part of Italy
rich in finds of Greek pottery, and the
very first vases they made included a
similar shape to the present vase,
decorated in 'encaustic' colours, imitating
the ancient 'red-figure' style (see cat. no.
46).

NOTE

1   Macht (1957) p. 62.

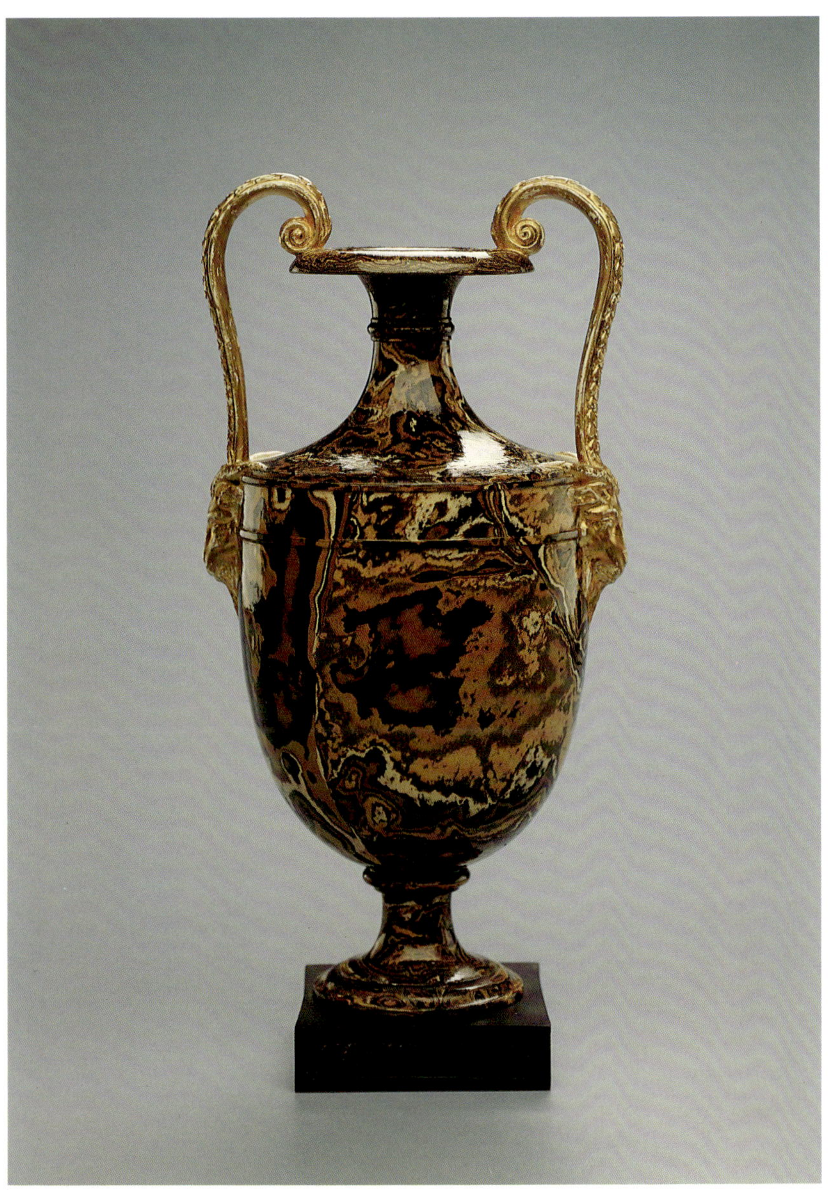

13 Vase and cover 1769–80

stoneware (basalt)
33.5 x 14.4 x 13.7 cm
Impressed mark on plinth: Wedgwood / &
Bentley
Presented through The Art Foundation of
Victoria by Mrs Norma Deutsher, Governor
1994   (D19-1994)

The shield-shaped vase has two
medallions showing nymphs in clouds, in
a style influenced by the recently
discovered decorations of ancient
Herculaneum near Naples. These are set
between floral swags. Above is a border
of figures among clouds, representing the
Loves of the Gods. The cover has, as a
finial, a seated figure of Apollo with his
lyre. The small handles at the shoulder
are partly fluted, like those found on
ancient bronzes.

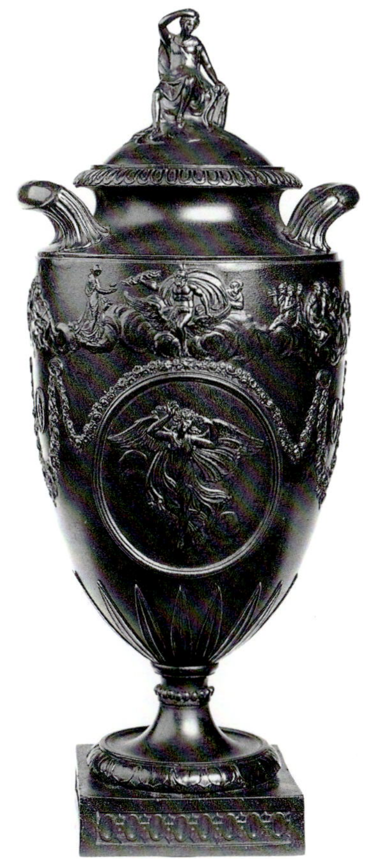

12 *Vase* 1769–80

earthenware (solid agate)
28.3 x 13.8 x 11.6 cm
Impressed mark on plinth: Wedgwood / &
Bentley
Presented through Art Foundation of Victoria
by Mrs Norma Deutsher, Governor 1992
(D9-1992)

The shield-shaped body of this vase is
formed from coloured clays wedged
together to simulate the patterning of
semi-precious stone. The tawny colour
of the body is offset by gilding applied to
the scrolling creamware handles which
rise from goat masks below the shoulder
of the vase and terminate at the flaring
mouth.

The ware known as 'agate', already in
use in Staffordshire for tea and table
wares, was particularly well suited to
Wedgwood's more sophisticated vase
shapes, making them resemble the stone
vases of wealthy collectors. Wedgwood's
gilding added to the richness of effect,
but was very fragile in the early period
(Wedgwood once even proposed that an
important commission be gilded after
delivery to avoid damage in transport).

The vase is marked with the name of
the partnership on the basalt plinth.
Although factory marks were in use at
this period, they were not common in
Staffordshire, and the Wedgwood and
Bentley partnership was unusual by any
standards in spelling out the name in full,
to enhance public awareness and
confound rival potters who might try to
make imitations.

14 *Medallion — Bacchanal*
1777–80

stoneware (blue jasper)
8.7 x 11.4 x 1.1 cm
Impressed mark: WEDGWOOD / &
BENTLEY
Presented through The Art Foundation of
Victoria by Mr Keith M. Deutsher, Founder
Benefactor 1993   (D8-1993)

The oval medallion shows a Bacchanal of
five *putti* and young satyrs, executed in
high relief in white. The classical subject
is seen through the eyes of the 17th
century. The source is François
Duquesnoy (also known as Il Fiammingo,
1594–1643).[1] Such a medallion was
suitable for inlaying in a fine cabinet.

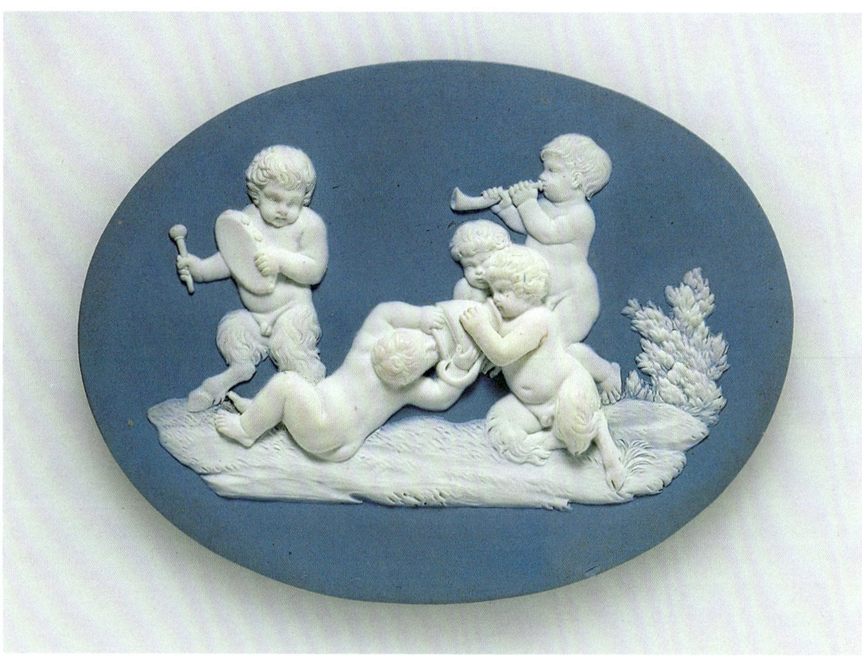

The development of jasper was the
outstanding technical achievement of the
Wedgwood and Bentley partnership (for
technical description see page 16, note
19). The material was developed to
harmonise with the style and light
colours of the Adam-style interior. It was
particularly inspired by antique carved
gemstones. 'Gems are the fountain head
of fine & beautiful composition, & we
cannot you know employ ourselves too
near the fountain head of taste',
Wedgwood wrote to Bentley as early as
1769.[2] He pursued his technical goal with
over 5000 recorded experiments, mostly
from December 1772 to December
1774, after which there were '4 black and

Blue onyx Intaglios' to be polished.[3] By
August 1775, Wedgwood wrote:

> I am going on a large scale with our
> Models &c which is one reason why
> you have so few new things just now,
> but I hope to bring the whole in
> compass for your next Winters shew
> & ASTONISH THE WORLD ALL AT
> ONCE.[4]

Jasper plaques did not appear in the
catalogues until 1777, though jasper was
made from about 1775.

The small plaque is gem-like in its fine
texture, the white relief being set on
solid greyish blue. The smooth front
surface, which appears a clearer blue,
seems to have been specially treated,
although no distinct layer of slip is visible.

Notes

1 The present group is part of a larger
   composition, given in Reilly (1989) vol. I,
   fig. 833 as Duquesnoy.
2 Farrer (1903) vol, I, p. 294.
3 Reilly (1989) vol. I, p. 524.
4 Farrer (1903) vol. 2, p. 239.

15 *Medallion — Dr Daniel*
Solander (1736–1782)
1775–80

Model by John Flaxman (1755–1826), 1775
stoneware (blue jasper)
8.4 x 7.0 x 1.3 cm
Impressed below bust: SOLANDER
Impressed mark: Wedgwood / & Bentley
Felton Bequest 1940   (4734-3)

The Swedish-born botanist Daniel
Charles Solander arrived in England in
1760 with the recommendation of
Linnaeus (the botanist responsible for the
modern classification of plants), and in
1767 accompanied Captain James Cook
on his voyage to the South Pacific in the
Endeavour. He travelled to Iceland in
1772 with Sir Joseph Banks and became
his secretary and librarian. In 1773 he
became Keeper of the Department of
Natural History at the British Museum.

This medallion of the Wedgwood and
Bentley period is one of the series of
portraits of 'Illustrious Moderns' which
the partners offered for sale to a public
anxious to collect images of their most
worthy and influential contemporaries.
Dr Solander is listed in the *Catalogue* of
1779, Class X, Section III, no 25, among
34 'Philosophers, Physicians, &c.',
including Sir William Hamilton and
'Captain Cooke'.

The portraits of Solander and Cook
are the earliest works known to have
been commissioned by Wedgwood from
the young sculptor John Flaxman, son of
Wedgwood's supplier of plaster casts, of
the same name (see also cat. no. 18 and
page 11).

This Wedgwood & Bentley medallion
is of a solid mottled grey–blue, the
surface appearing a slightly brighter blue,
and still exhibiting a slightly mottled
effect. Behind the relief two wide round
holes have been cut out to facilitate even
firing. This is characteristic of the early
medallions.

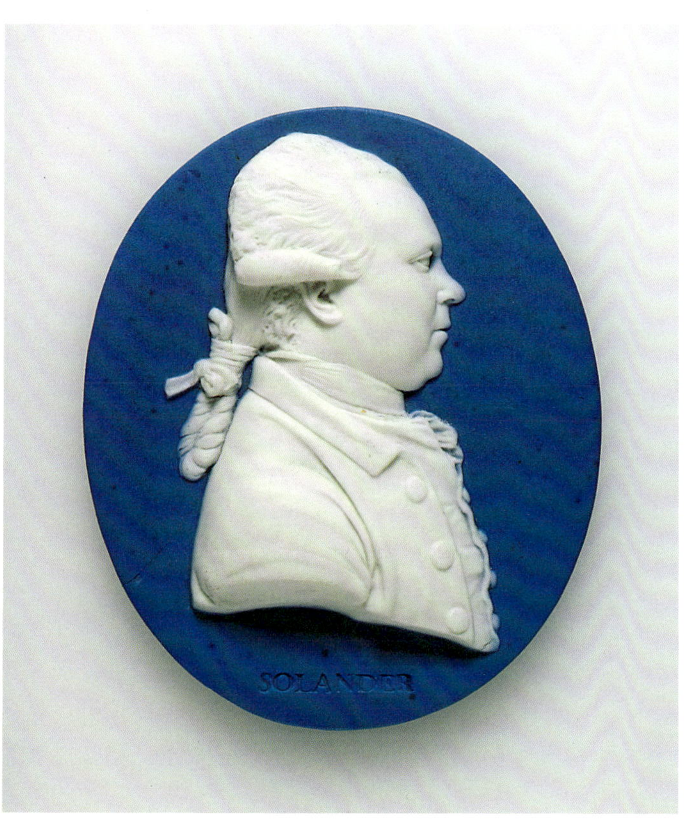

16 *Medallion — Empress
Catherine II of Russia
(1729–1796)* 1779–80

stoneware (basalt)
9.2 x 7.5 x 0.8 cm
Impressed mark: Wedgwood / & Bentley
Inscription below the portrait bust: EM.
RUSSIA
K. and N. Deutsher collection

Catherine was one of the most powerful
monarchs in Europe. She was an admirer
of English taste in architecture, gardens
and decoration, and one of Wedgwood's
major customers (see cat. nos 5 and 7).
She was also an important patron of
French decorative arts.

The medallion shows the empress
wrapped in ermine and with a dress of
scale armour crossed by a sash. She is
wearing a crown and a laurel wreath.
This miniature portrait in an integral
frame was moulded after a medal by
T. Ivanov, dated 1774. The extraordinary
detail of Wedgwood's basalt medallion,
notable in the minute rendering of the
scale pattern of the armour, rivals the
precision of works in metal. The
Catalogue of 1779, did not list a portrait
of Catherine, although Wedgwood had
written of the need for one in 1776.

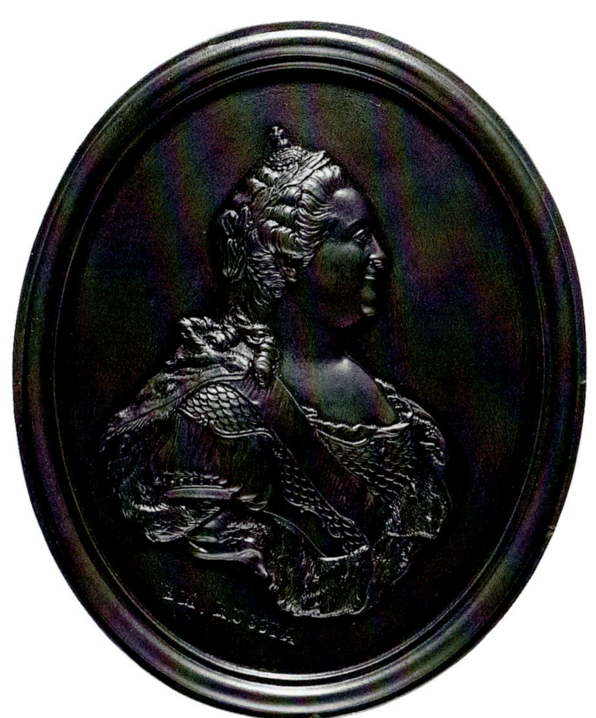

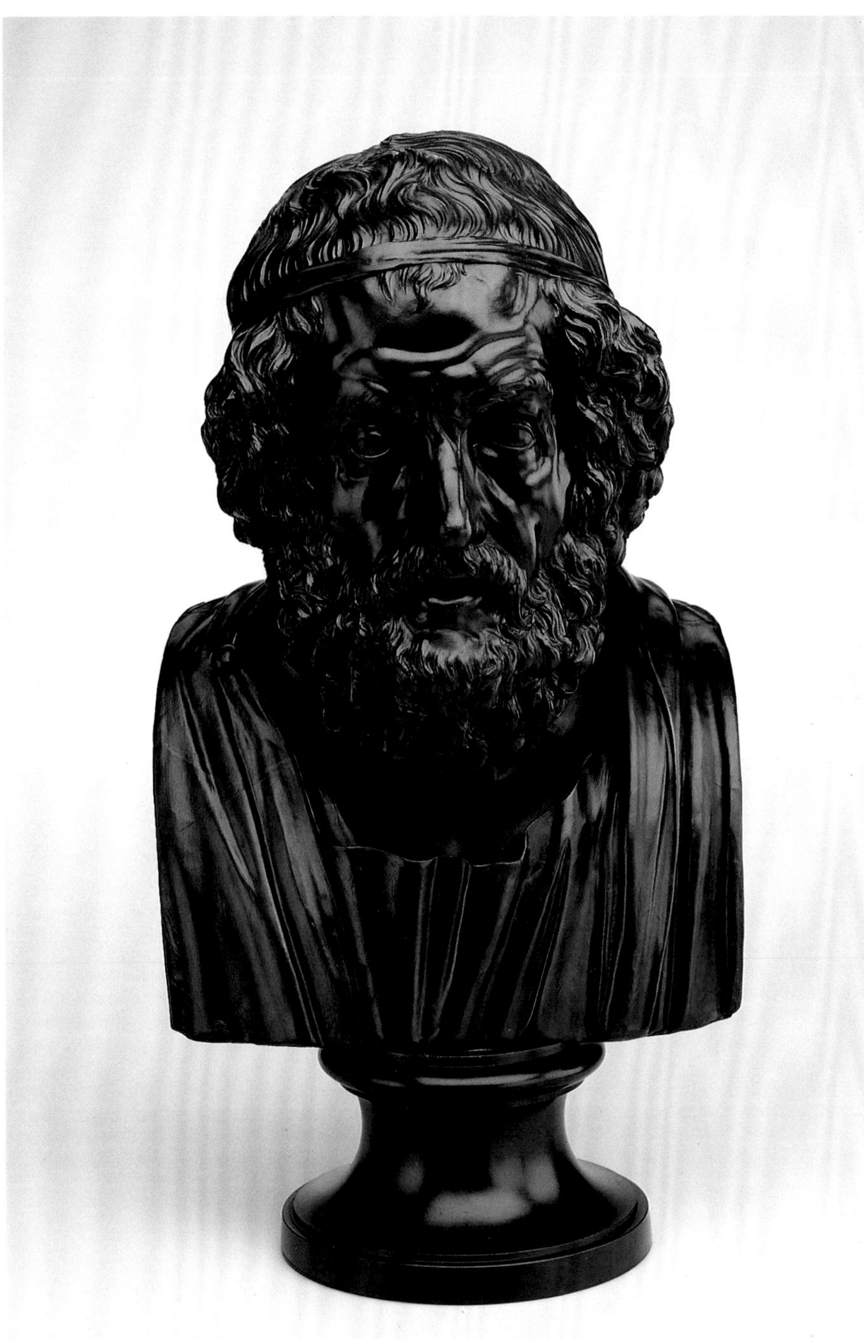

17 *Bust of Homer*
c. 1774–80

stoneware (basalt)
53.5 x 28.8 x 28.2 cm
Impressed mark on back of bust: HOMER /
Wedgwood / & Bentley
Impressed inside socle: WEDGWOOD / &
BENTLEY
K. and N. Deutsher collection

The large bust of Homer, set on a socle
base, was based on the antique marble
bust in the Farnese collection at Rome.[1]

No gentleman's house of the 18th
century was complete without a library
which underlined the owner's classical
education, and the ideal furnishing
included busts of the greatest classical or
modern authors. Set on top of the
shelves, the sculpted bust might be
framed by a broken pediment designed
by Sheraton or Chippendale, or set in a
niche above a built-in Adam bookcase.

Wedgwood & Bentley began to supply
this market with busts in the basalt body
which had the 'Appearance of Antique

Bronze'. While only three busts (Cicero,
Horace and George II) were offered in
their 1773 *Catalogue*, the number was
greatly expanded in the following years
until 87 different designs, including men
of science as well as literary figures, were
listed in the 1779 *Catalogue*.

The prototypes were generally
supplied by makers of plaster casts after
ancient and contemporary sculptures.
The *Homer* was supplied by John Cheere
(1709–87) in 1774. He was the brother
of the accomplished sculptor Henry
Cheere and had a business in plaster
library busts, garden statuary and
classical figures, sometimes designing
himself some whimsical figures in Rococo
taste. His sculpture yard at Hyde Park
Corner is the subject of an engraving by
William Hogarth.[2]

Fired clay press-moulds were made
from the model, and initially these were
also made outside the factory. But on
16 August 1774 Wedgwood wrote to
Bentley:

> You will find our Busts much finer &
> better finish'd than the Plaister ones
> we take them from — Hackwood
> bestows a week upon each head in
> restoring it to what we suppose it
> was when it came out of the hands of
> the Statuary. Pray do not let our
> labour be unobserv'd …[3]

In all, the Wedgwood & Bentley bust
of the blind poet does credit to the
expressive ancient work from which it
derives.

NOTES

1   The Farnese collection is now in the
    National Archaeological Museum at
    Naples.
2   See Hogarth (1753) in which the stiff
    deportment of his day is contrasted with
    the graceful posture of antique statues.
    See also *The Man at Hyde Park Corner*
    (1974).
3   Farrer (1903) vol. 2, p. 190. For
    Hackwood, see cat. no. 35.

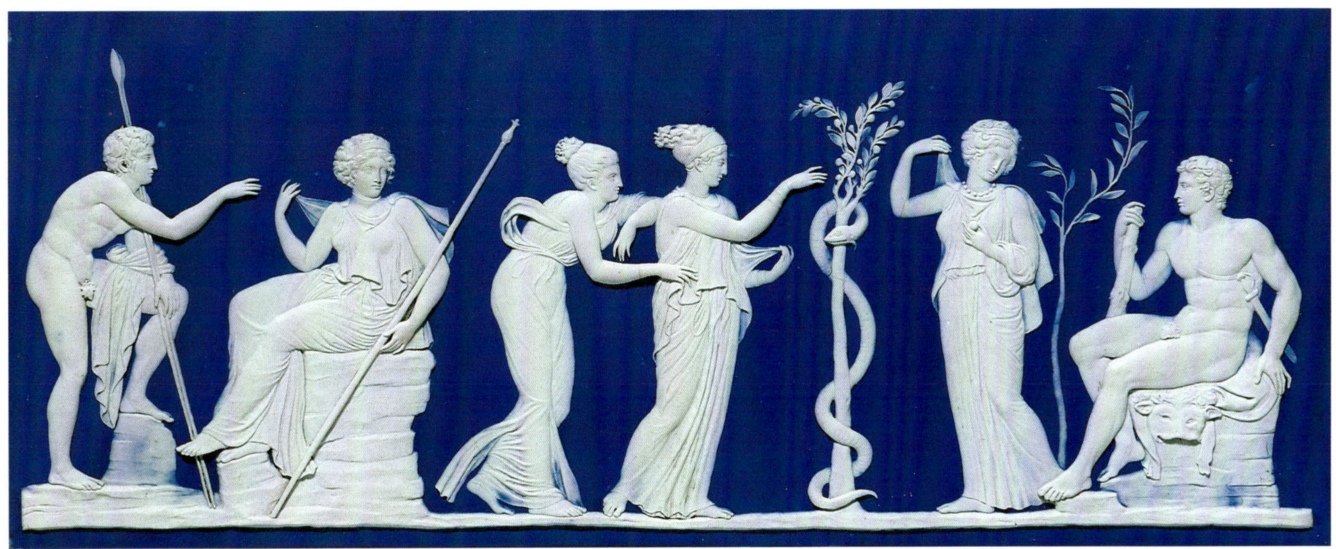

18 *Plaque — Hercules in the Garden of the Hesperides 1787–95*

Model by John Flaxman (1755–1826), 1785–87
stoneware (blue jasper)
36.1 x 14.9 x 1.0 cm
Impressed mark: WEDGWOOD
Purchased 1877   (231-1)

This fine relief was listed in the 1787 *Catalogue* as 'From a beautiful Etruscan vase in the collection of Sir William Hamilton, now in the British Museum'. In preparing the model the young John Flaxman achieved a very fine style, preserving the best of the antique and subtly improving upon the rhythms of the original while translating it into three dimensions.[1]

The design, which appears on a Greek red-figure vase of the late 5th century BC by the Meidias Painter, had been published by d'Hancarville in vol. II (pl. 74). The published design was adjusted to a rectangular format, and surrounded by an ornamental border which was freely adapted from ancient vase painting.

The Gallery's plaque is in lapis blue jasper dip over solid greyish blue. It was purchased from the widow of Augustus Henry Tulk (1810–73), son of Charles Augustus Tulk (1786–1849), a friend of John Flaxman and former owner of a Wedgwood first edition *Portland vase* now in the British Museum. From 1856 the younger Tulk was the energetic and enlightened librarian of the Melbourne public library. He also worked for the establishment of an art gallery in the colony, which would lead in time to the establishment of the National Gallery of Victoria.

John Flaxman first exhibited at the Royal Academy in 1770, when he was only fifteen, and supplied many designs for Wedgwood early in his career before leaving for Rome in 1787. There he supervised a team of sculptors engaged by Wedgwood to copy the best antiques. He was the leading Neoclassical sculptor of his age, capable of tender expression allied to compositions chaste to the point of severity. His work is distinguished by a particularly fine sense of the harmonious interval. His line drawings of subjects from Homer, published in engraved form in 1793, are among the most radical expressions of the Neoclassical ideal, and were widely admired. He was appointed professor of sculpture at the Royal Academy in 1810.

NOTE

1   The design was first discussed in a letter from Flaxman to Wedgwood, 20 October 1785, and invoiced, at £23, in August 1787. Despite a certain artistic independence, Flaxman has preserved the odd curved lines which cut across the vertical folds of drapery at the waists of the female figures. On the original Greek vase these lines represented drapery folds but here, following d'Hancarville, they look like added strings. The Gallery's relief has a number of small firing holes (for ventilation) at the back.

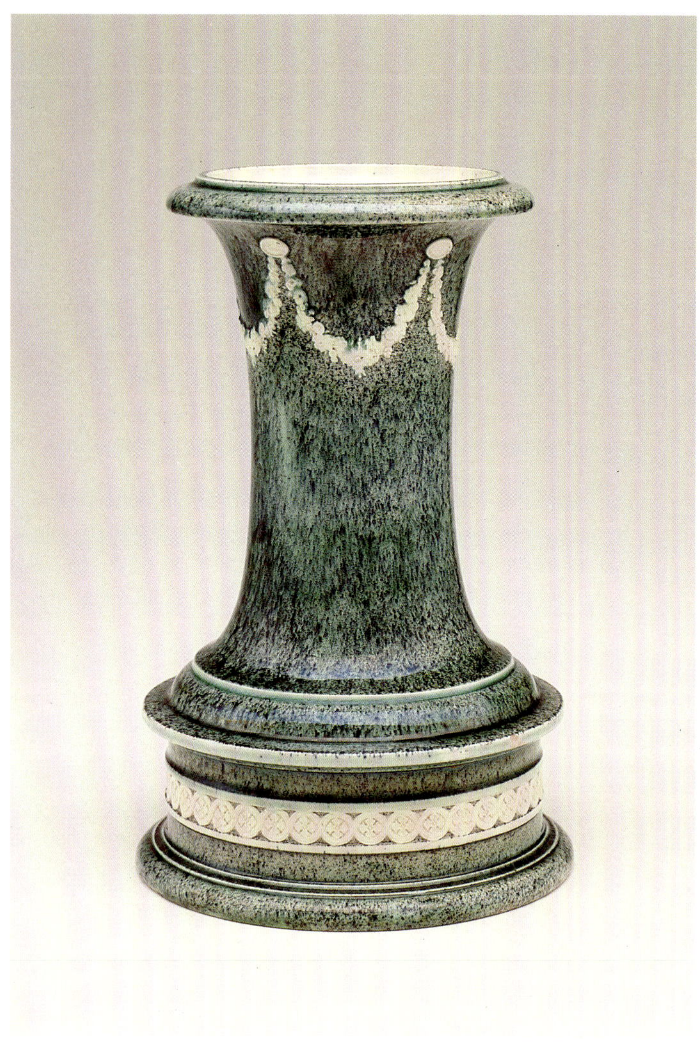

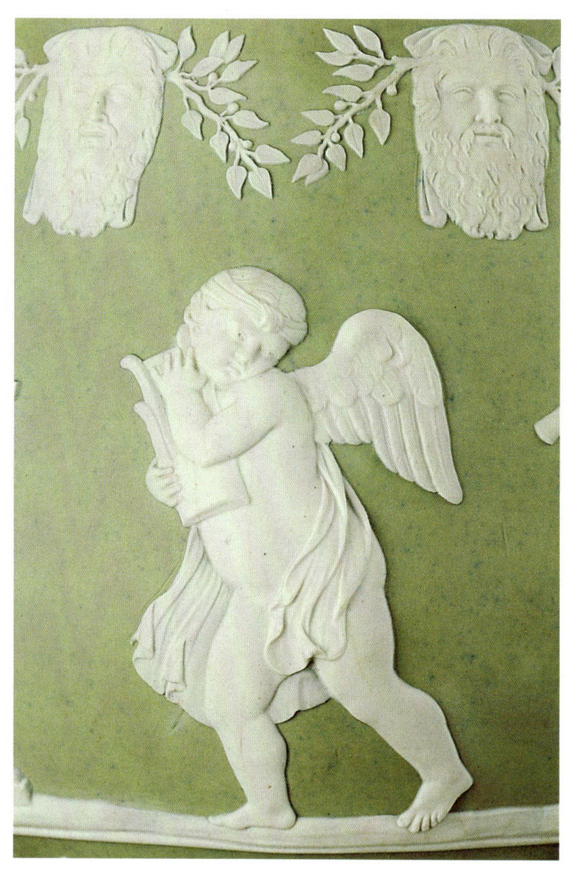

20 *Vase (bough-pot)*
c. 1785–1800

stoneware (green jasper wash)
28.6 x 16.4 x 16.4 cm
Impressed mark: WEDGWOOD
Presented through The Art Foundation of
Victoria by Mrs Norma Deutsher, Governor
1993   (D21-1993)

19 *Vase* 1785–90

stoneware (white terracotta)
20.6 x 13.1 x 13.1 cm
Impressed mark: WEDGWOOD
Gift of Mr Frank Sweett 1994

The mallet-shaped vase has floral
garlands in relief on the concave column
section of the body and a band of
guilloche pattern enclosing rosettes
around the drum-like lower part. The
ornaments have been left in white against
a variegated green glaze imitating stone
(green porphyry).[1] The inside of the rim
is shaped to take a flat perforated lid.

NOTES

1   Traces of gilding are sometimes found on
    the white reliefs of this class.
2   Cf. Rathbone (1898) pl. XXXVIII, where
    the shape is described as a hyacinth pot.

The baluster-shaped vase has a semi-
transparent wash of green jasper. It is
decorated with eight winged boys as
musicians, with a band of bearded masks
and delicate leaves above, an antique
design which comes from a Roman urn in
the Capitoline Museum.[1] Below are
ornaments of stiff leaves and
honeysuckle, while at the rim is a border
of anthemion. The vase is supported on a
waisted socle and set on a square, off-
white base. It has a flat, pierced cover,
designed to preserve the arrangement of
flowers.

NOTE

1   A wax model for the relief is preserved at
    Port Sunlight, England. See Reilly (1989)
    vol. I, fig. 941a.

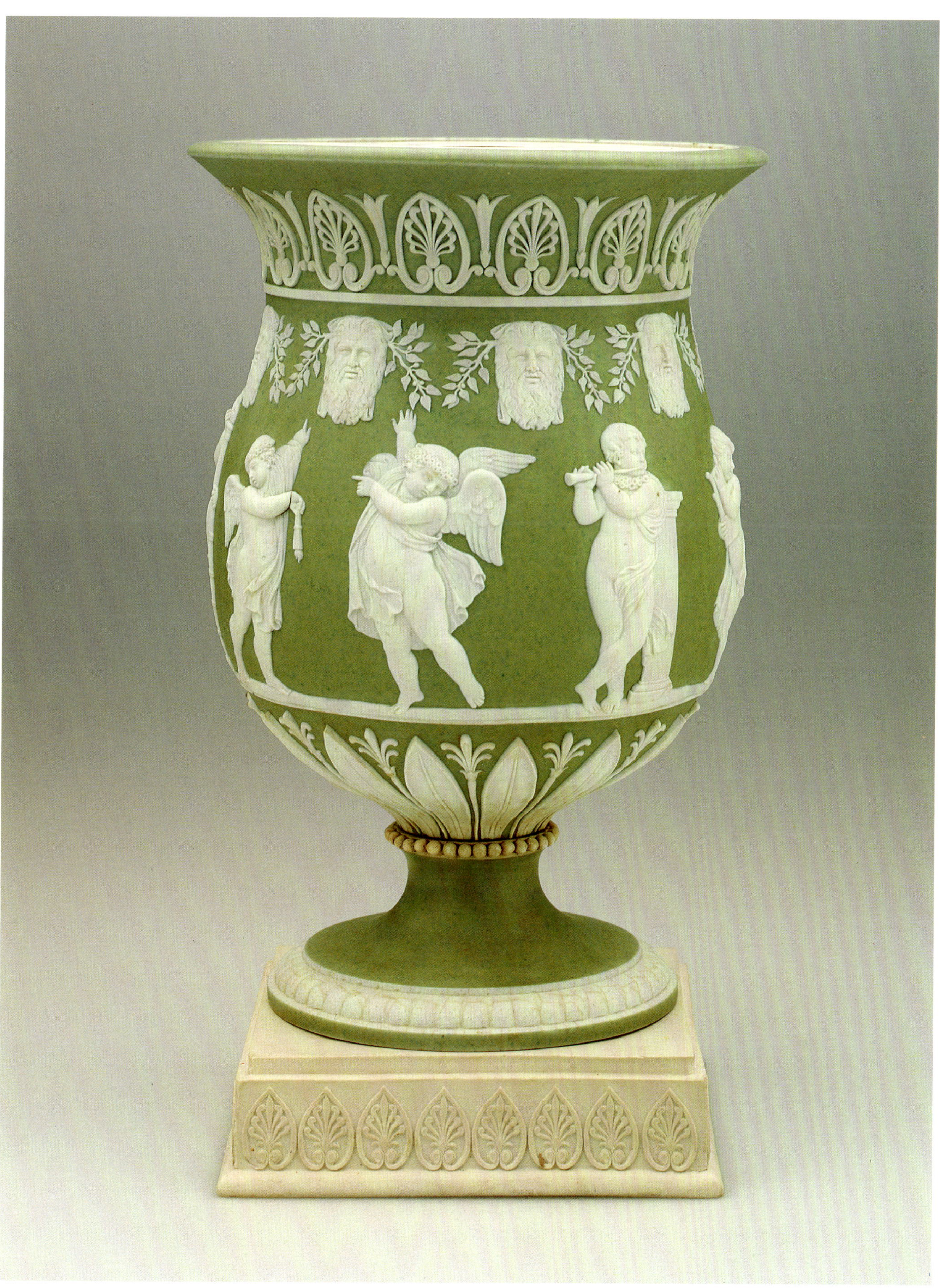

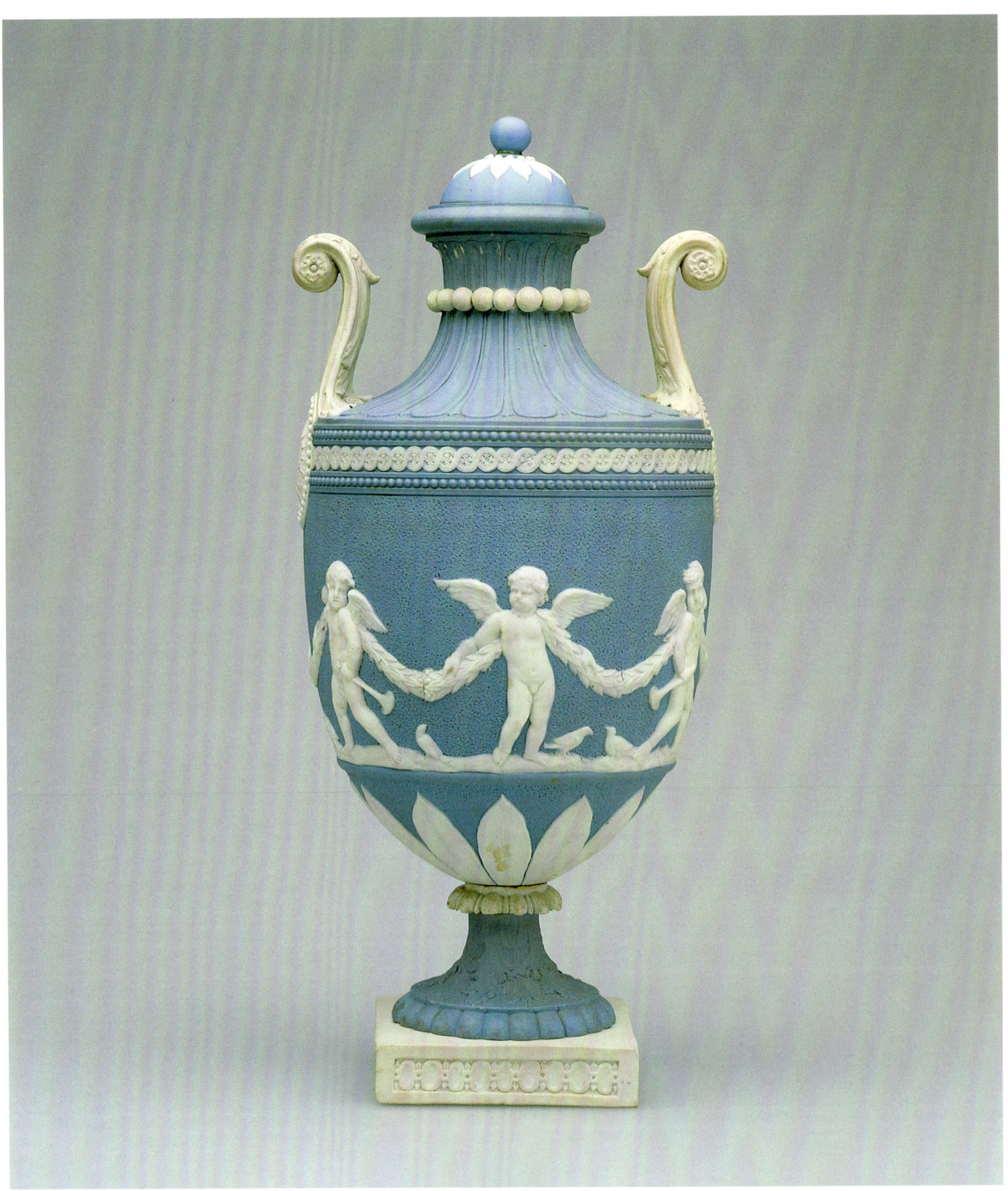

21 *Vase* c. 1785

stoneware (blue jasper)
20.5 x 10.3 x 10.1 cm (22.7 cm with
replacement stopper)
Impressed mark: WEDGWOOD
K. and N. Deutsher collection

The shield-shaped vase is encircled by a band of winged *putti* supporting a continuous garland. It is an ancient motif which effectively combines repetition and variety. There are doves at the boys' feet. The solid blue vase has a 'dimpled' (orange-peel textured) ground, upright scroll handles set above paterae, and a socle-shaped foot, richly moulded with acanthus. It is set on a square white jasper base with ovolo moulding. There are applied white beads at the neck, and a roulette[1] has been used to make the smaller-scale bead patterns which flank a guilloche border just below the shoulder.

The vase is shown with an appropriate but later stopper with 'stiff leaf' decoration.

NOTE

1   The roulette is a small wheel with a pattern carved into its edge so that it creates a band of ornament as it rolls over the clay.

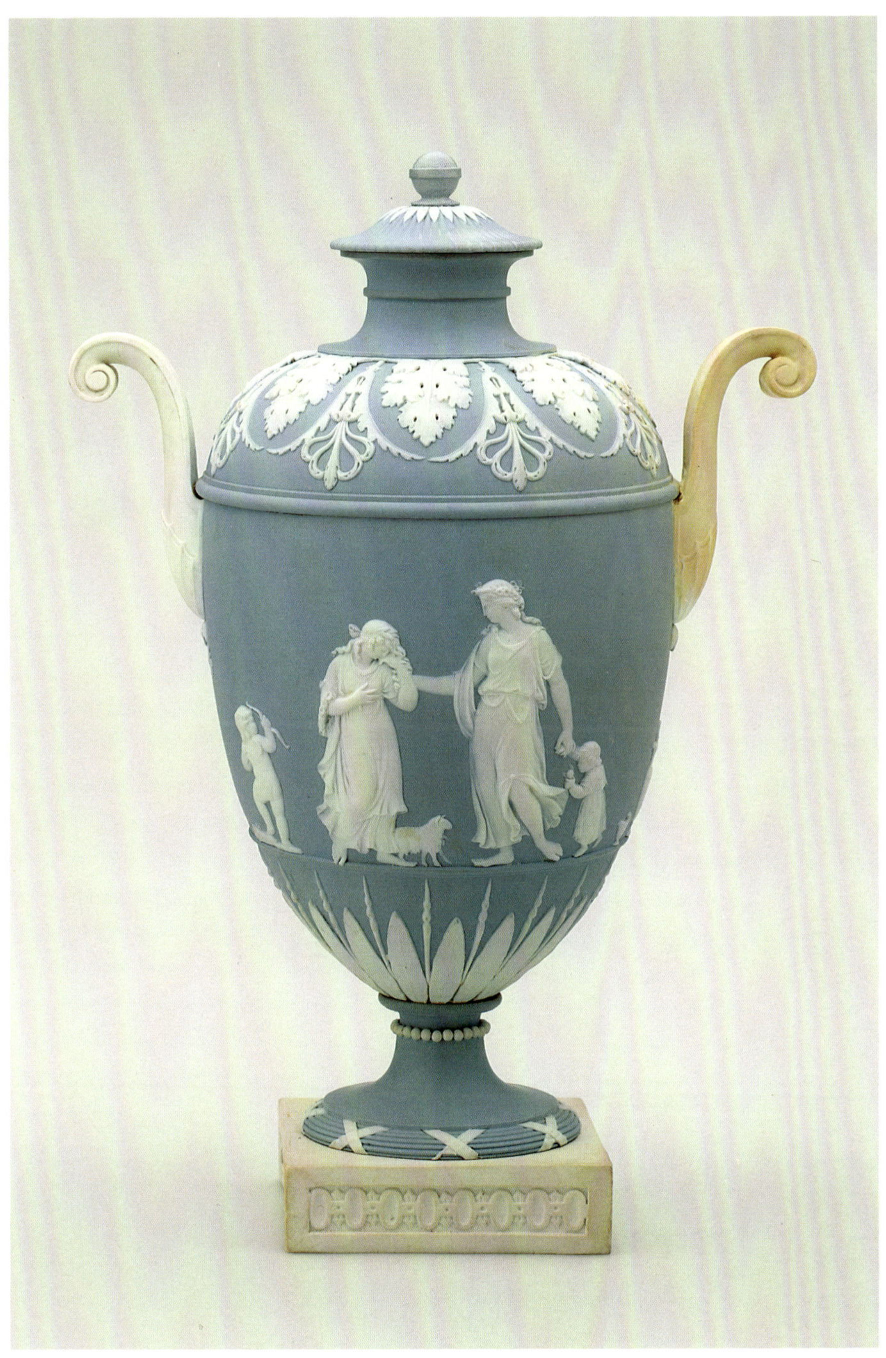

22 *Vase and cover* c. 1785

stoneware (blue jasper)
27.0 x 18.5 x 12.4 cm
Impressed mark: WEDGWOOD
K. and N. Deutsher collection

The ovoid vase has short outward-scrolling handles in white attached with a fan-like fluted motif below a rich band of acanthus leaves and stylised palmettes covering the shoulder. The body shows a section of the relief called 'An offering to Peace' designed by Lady Templetown, and on the other side is an unusual landscape design consisting of a clump of trees sheltering some sheep. In addition there are delicately modelled flowers growing, and a dragonfly makes a delicious detail.

Below is a band of stiff leaves and darts. There is applied beading at the junction of the socle foot, which is finished with a reed-bundle border. The square white jasper base has a type of ovolo moulding. The lid has radiating ribs, and an applied white line around the spherical finial. There was a particularly careful elaboration of ornament at this time.

Elizabeth, Lady Templetown (1747-1823) created designs in a manner well suited to the age of sentiment. The charm of childhood and the virtues of family life, were newly rediscovered, and all that was good was seen as stemming from nature and natural affections. This aristocratic amateur painter and sculptor supplied designs to Wedgwood as drawings and in 'cut Indian paper' (silhouettes) between 1783 and 1789.

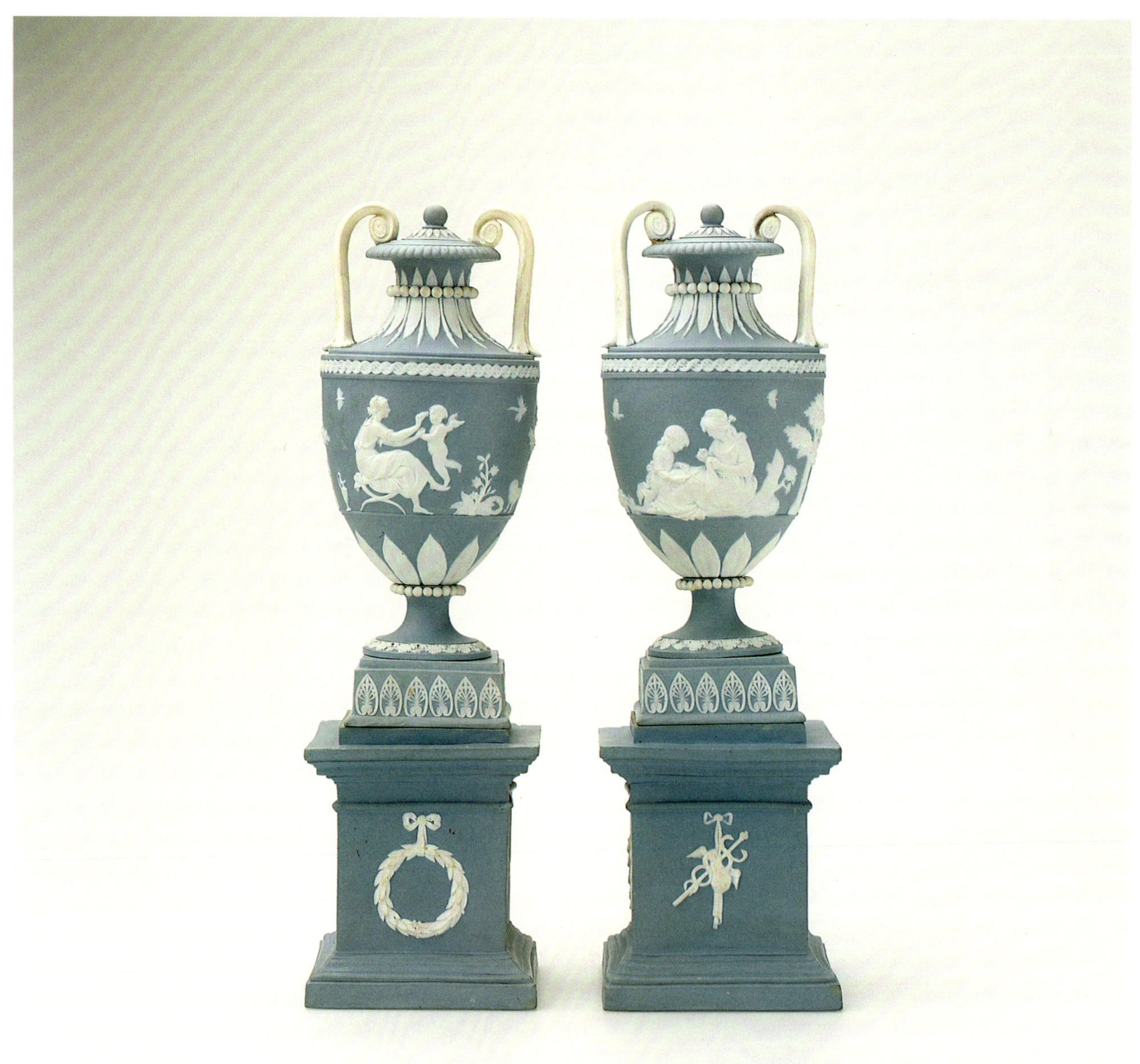

23 *Pair of covered vases and pedestals* c. 1790

stoneware (blue jasper)
vases 17.6 x 7.6 x 7.5 cm
pedestals 9.4 x 7.8 x 7.8 cm
overall height 26.7 cm
Impressed mark on each: WEDGWOOD
Presented through The Art Foundation of
Victoria by Mrs Norma Deutsher, Governor
1994 (D23-1994)

These very unusual miniature vases bear
the fittingly intimate subjects of Lady
Templetown's 'Domestic employments'
and 'Sportive love' designs and another
of similar type which appears to be 'The

sewing lesson' listed as by the amateur
artist Emma Crewe (active 1787–1818).
The fourth subject is 'Charlotte at the
tomb of Werther' (see cat. no. 24).

The vases are made in solid blue
jasper, apart from the white scrolling
handles and applied beading at neck and
foot. The plinth attached to each vase is
blue-dipped white jasper. The solid blue
jasper pedestals are decorated in relief
with garlands and trophies which
represent the winged thunderbolt of Jove
and the *caduceus* (wand) and purse of
Mercury, patron of commerce.

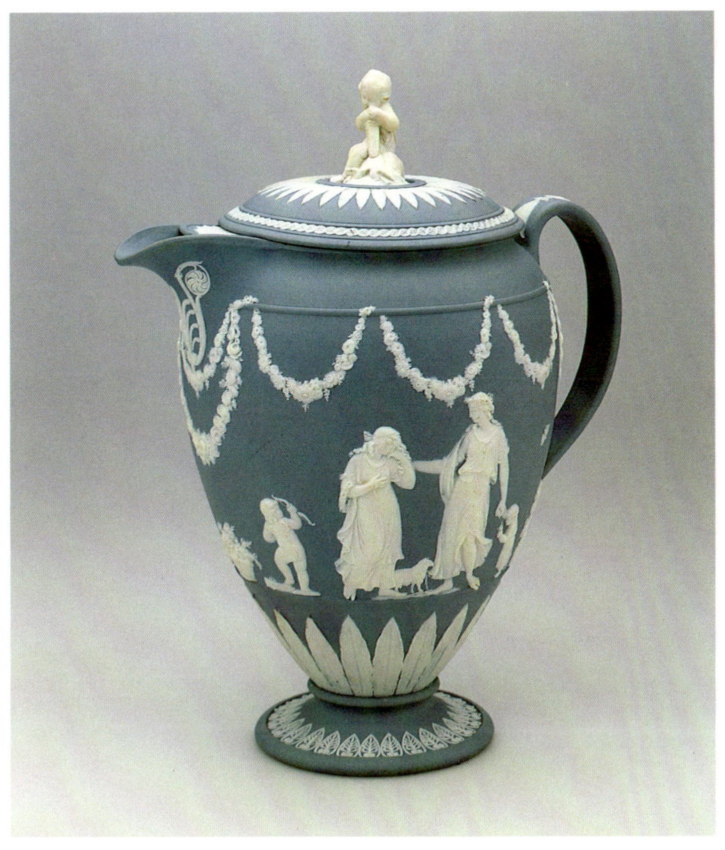

24 *Coffee pot* c. 1790

stoneware (blue jasper)
24.7 x 20.1 x 13.8 cm
Impressed mark: WEDGWOOD
Incised: 王
K. and N. Deutsher collection

The coffee pot has an inverted pear-shaped body on a socle foot. A figure of Cupid provides the finial for the lid which has radiating 'stiff leaves'. The reliefs on the body were designed by Lady Templetown and depict a group from her design, 'An offering to Peace', and on the other side 'Charlotte at the tomb of Werther'. The girl kneeling before an urn illustrates the theme of the popular novel of sentiment, *The Sorrows of Young Werther*. This early work of the great German poet and Romantic theorist Goethe (1749–1832) became a sort of cult icon, and was blamed for many suicides over unrequited love. The relief was modelled by William Hackwood (see cat. no. 35).

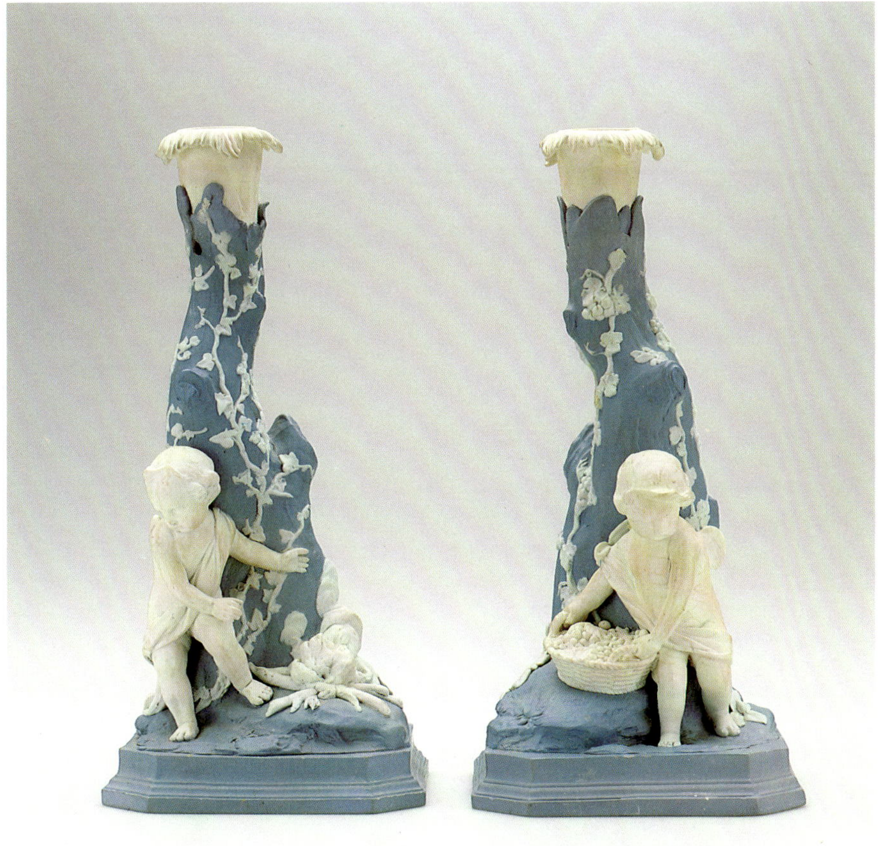

25 *Pair of candlesticks —*
Autumn and Winter
c. 1785

stoneware (blue jasper)
Autumn 28.0 x 12.9 x 13.0 cm
Winter 27.1 x 12.7 x 13.0 cm
Impressed mark on both: WEDGWOOD
K. and N. Deutsher collection

Autumn is represented by a winged *putto* carrying a basket of fruit, and Winter by another who is warming his hands beside a fire. The candleholders are naturalistically modelled as tree trunks, Autumn with a trailing grapevine and Winter with ivy, and set on a square base.[1] The Rococo forms and rustic subject matter of these candlesticks in solid blue and white jasper are most unusual for Wedgwood, being close in spirit to porcelain figures of the 1760s. The candlesticks are rare and no models of Spring or Summer are known.

NOTE

1   The traditional attribution of this model to William Hackwood is uncertain.

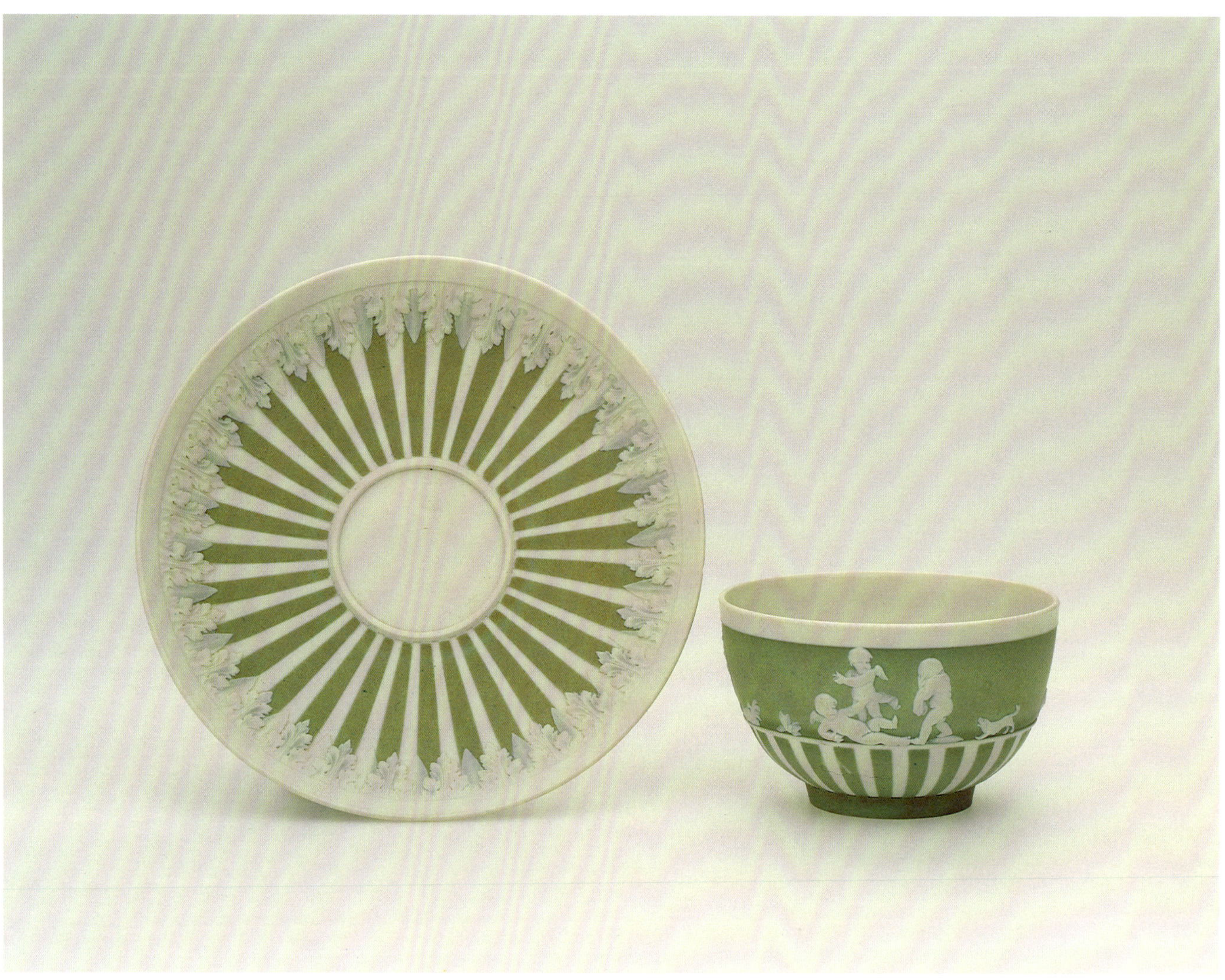

26 *Teabowl and saucer* c. 1790

stoneware (green jasper dip)
teabowl 4.5 x 7.5 x 7.5 cm
saucer 2.3 x 12.8 x 12.8 cm
Impressed mark on both pieces:
WEDGWOOD / 3
Presented through The Art Foundation of
Victoria by Mrs Norma Deutsher, Governor
1993   (D22-1993)

The teabowl in green jasper dip is
decorated with children at play, after a
design by Lady Templetown. Vertical
green and white stripes below have been
made by engine-turning, and the saucer
has similar engine-turning and an
acanthus leaf border in relief. The high
polish of the interior of the bowl was
almost certainly achieved using lapidary
(gem-cutting) techniques. At times,
however, the fire itself could produce a
fine, glossy surface.

27 *Wine cooler* c. 1790

stoneware (green jasper dip with yellow)
26.3 x 28.3 x 23.3 cm
Impressed mark: WEDGWOOD
Presented through The Art Foundation of
Victoria by Mr Keith M. Deutsher, Founder
Benefactor 1993   (D13-1993)

The barrel-shaped vessel has swan-neck
handles terminating in spreading wings,
and is decorated with a band of male and
female banqueters reclining in the antique
manner. The figures are set in a central
band between areas of dice pattern with
cane yellow quatrefoils in the white
squares. The predominating green is an
unusual olive–buff colour.

   The 'Banqueters' design was
prepared for Wedgwood by Giuseppe
Angelini in Rome in 1789,[1] and was
modelled after the *Sarcophagus of the
Muses*.[2] The wine cooler is one of the
largest pieces of dice-pattern jasper

made. The dice pattern consists of a
design of squares made by cutting
through the top layer of coloured jasper.
This was done by engine-turning on a
lathe.[3]

NOTES

1   Reilly (1989) vol. II, p. 603.
2   The *Sarcophagus of the Muses*, formerly in
    the Albani collection and the Capitoline
    Museum, is now in the Louvre. It was
    illustrated in Montfaucon (1722) vol. I, pl.
    LIX.
3   The lathe, also known as a 'rose-engine',
    is investigated in detail in Adeney (1989).
    See also page 9.

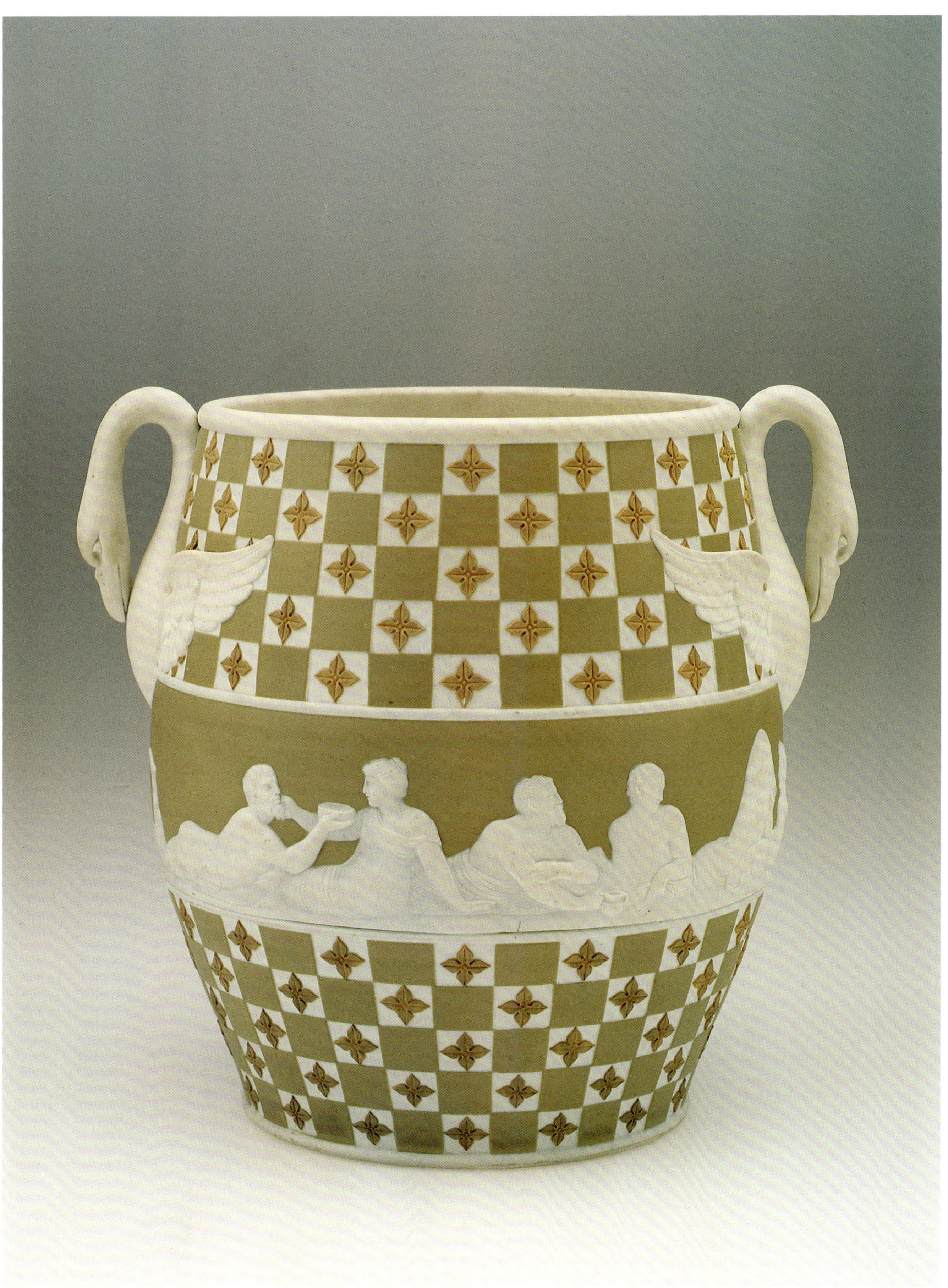

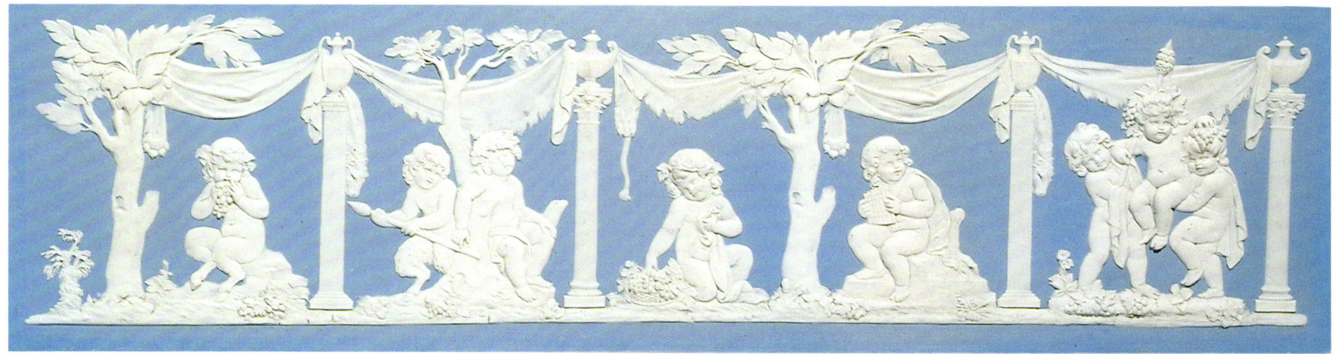

28 *Plaque — Bacchanalian Boys* c. 1790

After a design by Lady Diana Beauclerc
(1734–1808)
Stoneware (blue jasper)
15.6 x 58.8 cm
Impressed mark: WEDGWOOD
Presented through The Art Foundation of
Victoria by Mrs Norma Deutsher, Governor
1994   (D38-1994)

The solid blue plaque, or 'tablet' as it would have been called in the 18th century, shows young boys at play, as musicians and Bacchic revellers, the subject divided into five panels by trees and columns supporting panther skins.

The designer of the subject, Lady Diana Beauclerc (1734–1808), born Lady Spencer, eldest daughter of the Duke of Marlborough, belonged to literary circles and was a friend of Dr Johnson. As an artist she is known especially for her drawings of children. Some of her designs, including the group of three boys seen on the present plaque, were also engraved by Francesco Bartolozzi.

Wedgwood gratefully received one of her designs at least as early as 1785. William Hackwood translated them into Wedgwood reliefs, and her work appears in the 1787 *Catalogue,* which acknowledges her 'exquisite Taste'. Her groups of playful children were available separately and were also combined in a composite 'Bacchanalian tablet' of boys 'under arbours, with panthers' skins in festoons'.

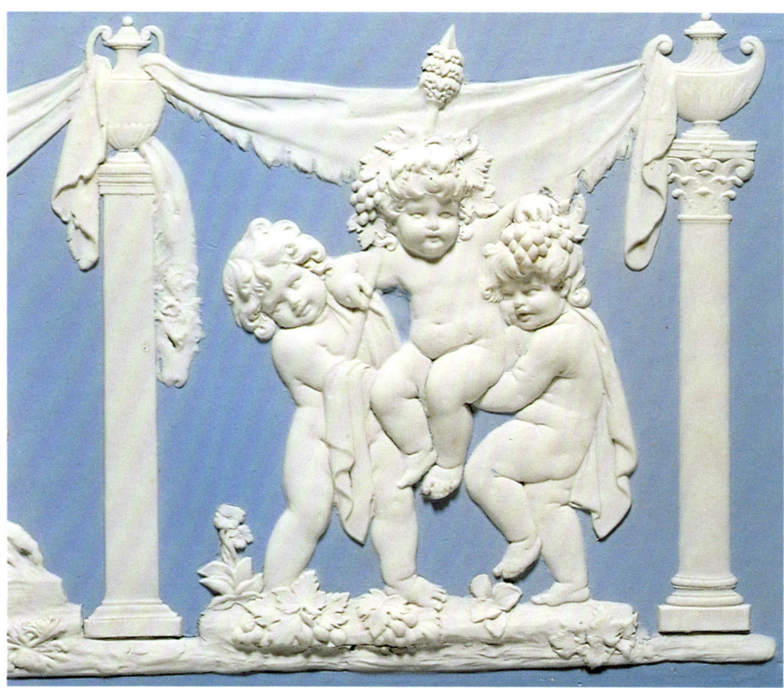

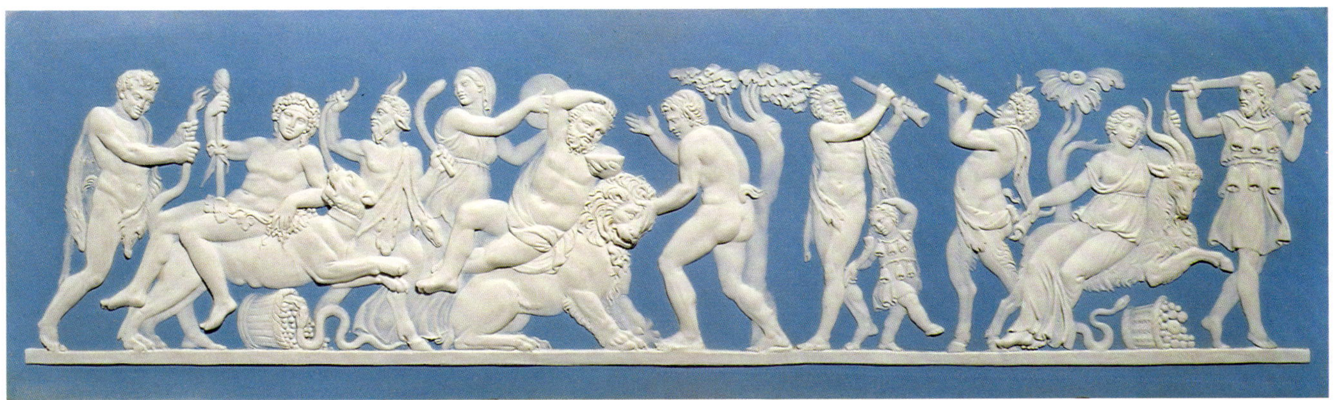

29 *Plaque — Triumph of Bacchus*
probably late 18th century

stoneware (blue jasper)
15.2 x 51.0 cm
Impressed mark: WEDGWOOD
Presented through The Art Foundation of
Victoria by Mrs Norma Deutsher, Governor
1994   (D37-1994)

The plaque shows a triumphal procession
with the god Bacchus seated on a
panther, Silenus riding a lion, and a
woman (possibly Ariadne) seated on a
goat. They are accompanied by a faun
twisting the tail of the panther, a horned
satyr, a woman with a drum in her hand,
a musician, a dancing child wearing a
bizarre costume of bells, and a man in a
similar costume, carrying a club and a
small goat.

The source of the design is a Roman
sarcophagus in the Capitoline Museum.
The relief is very vigorously modelled,
perhaps by Pacetti (see cat. no. 36C)
working under John Flaxman at Rome.

The surface of the solid blue jasper
plaque is unusually smooth and highly
vitrified.[1]

NOTE

1   Cf. a green jasper plaque *Birth of Bacchus*
    in the Wedgwood Museum, Barlaston,
    illustrated in Reilly (1989) vol. I, pl. C156.
    Reilly refers to Wedgwood's mention of a
    surface 'glaze' in a letter of 10 March
    1776.

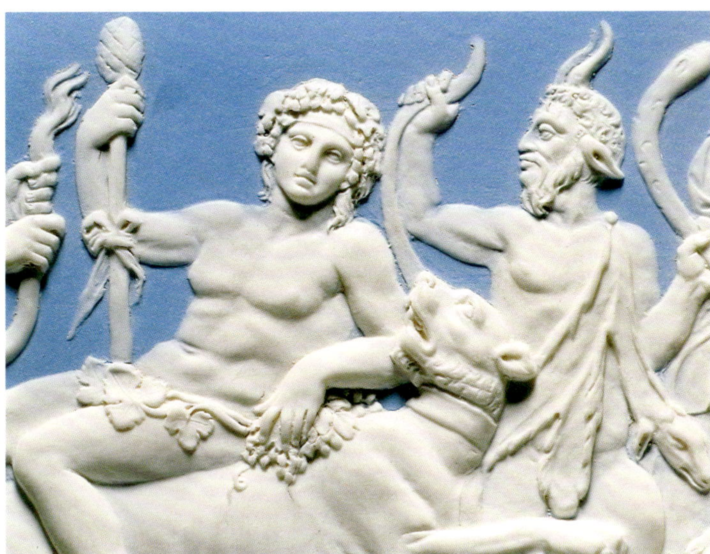

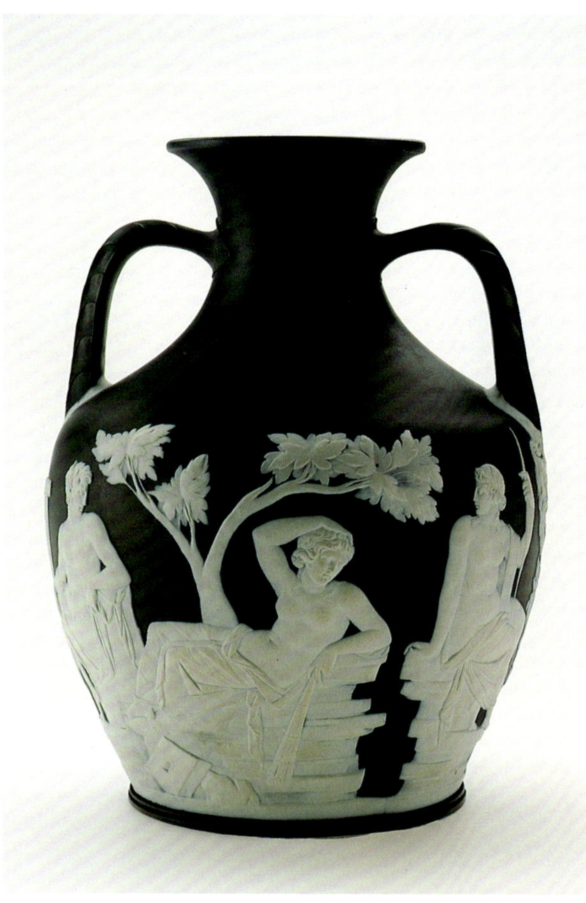

30 *Portland vase* c. 1791

stoneware (blue–black jasper)
24.7 x 19.0 x 19.0 cm
Unmarked
Presented through The Art Foundation of
Victoria by Mr Keith Deutsher, Governor
1992 (D8-1992)

Wedgwood's *Portland* vases reproduce
the famous classical cameo glass vase
which was once in the Barberini family in
Rome and then purchased from Sir
William Hamilton by the Duchess of
Portland.[1] This is a work from around
the time of the emperor Augustus
(27 BC–AD 14), made in Alexandria or
Rome. It is now in the British Museum,
to which institution John Wedgwood
gave a mid-blue first edition copy in 1802.

It was probably John Flaxman who
first alerted Josiah I Wedgwood to the
antique vase then in Sir William
Hamilton's possession in London. On
5 February 1784 he wrote:

> ... it is the finest production of Art
> that has been brought to England
> and seems to be the very apex of
> perfection to which you are

endeavouring to bring
your bisque and
jasper; ... engraved
in the same manner
as a Cameo & of the
grandest & most
perfect Greek
sculpture.

Wedgwood began
work from the
illustration published by
Montfaucon, which had
hardly done justice to
the vase. Then, in 1786,
as soon as the Duke of
Portland had the vase,
he made it available to
Wedgwood to copy.

Josiah Wedgwood's
Portland vase was in
many ways his master-
work, calling on his
utmost powers as
artist, chemist, potter
and entrepreneur. The
project was financed by
subscription, as major
book publishing is
sometimes financed.
The first successful
example was shown to
Queen Charlotte in 1790 and also to Sir
Joshua Reynolds, President of the Royal
Academy, so that he might approve it as a
faithful copy. It was then exhibited in
Holland and Germany.

When Wedgwood made the reliefs he
was assisted by his son Josiah II, and by
the modellers William Hackwood (see
cat. no. 35) and Henry Webber
(1754–1826). Webber, the son of a Swiss
sculptor, trained at the Royal Academy
and joined Wedgwood in 1782. He was
head of Wedgwood's ornamental works
at Etruria 1785–1806, and travelled to
Rome to work for Wedgwood in 1787.[2]

Several sets of reliefs were made
before Wedgwood was satisfied, and a
long series of experiments was
undertaken in order to develop the
desired blue–black jasper body which
would imitate the dark-blue glass of the
original and to create the transparent
effect of glass:

> My present difficulty is to give those
> beautiful shades to the thin and
> distant parts of the figures, for which
> the original artist availed himself of
> the semitransparency of the white

glass, cutting it down nearer and
nearer to the blue ground in
proportion as he wished to increase
the depth of shade. But ... I must
depend upon ... the action of fire on
my compositions: a little more or a
little less fire, and even the length of
time employed in producing the same
degree, will make a very material
difference in this delicate operation.[3]

About forty-five examples were made
of the first edition, the only one made in
the lifetime of Josiah I. Thirty-nine
surviving examples are known, including
damaged and imperfectly fired ones.[4]

The present blue–black copy has the
silky surface and the characteristic
proportions of the first edition, although
the relief is not so transparent as
Wedgwood had desired. It has no flaws in
the firing.

The base of the vase is decorated in
relief and shows a half-figure of a man
wearing an Oriental headdress (see
illustration page 11).

NOTES

1   The vase was known to the collector
    Nicolas de Peiresc in 1600. It was in the
    collection of the Barberini family in Rome,
    then briefly in the possession of Sir
    William Hamilton, and was sold to the
    Duchess of Portland in 1784. After her
    death, her son the Duke paid 980 guineas
    for it at auction in 1786. Identification of
    the subject of the reliefs on the vase is a
    matter of lively debate. The relief appears
    to be in elegiac mood: the central figure
    on one side is shown with an inverted
    torch, the symbol of death. The ancient
    disc which forms the base of the vase was
    added before 1600.
2   Roberts (1986a) pp. 215–27.
3   Wedgwood to Sir William Hamilton
    (draft) 16 June 1787, see Finer & Savage
    (1965) pp. 307–8.
4   Dawson (1984) pp. 149–50. The Deutsher
    blue–black copy was acquired from
    D. Bernheim in 1974. It was sold by
    Christie's, London, 1 June 1970.

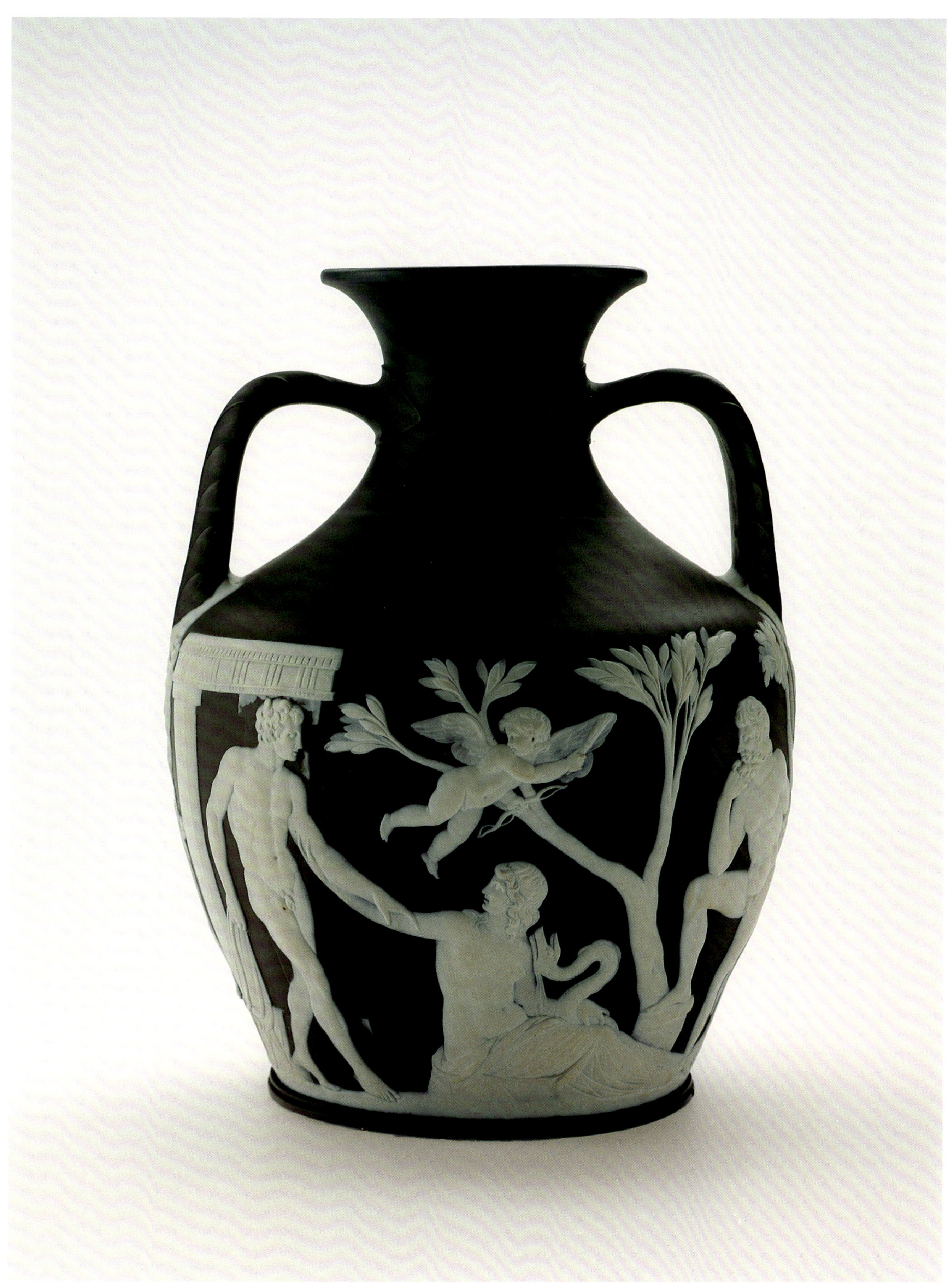

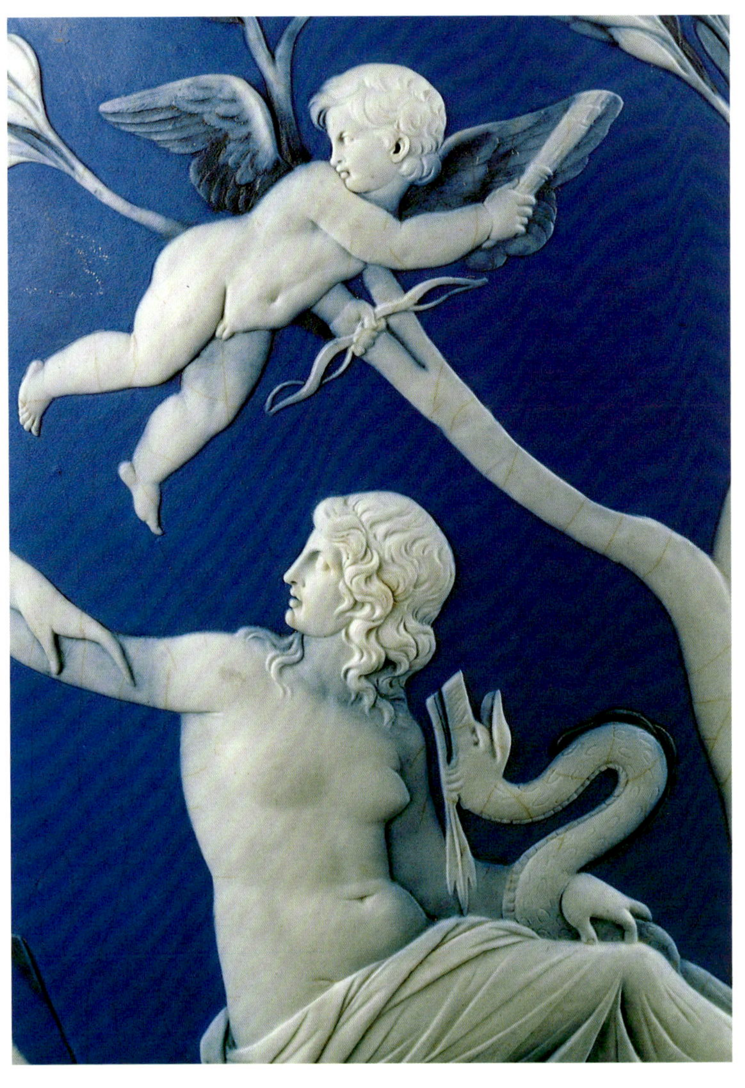

31 *Portland vase* c. 1791

stoneware (blue jasper dip on slate-grey)
26.4 x 18.7 x 18.7 cm
Unmarked
K. and N. Deutsher collection

The mid-blue copy of the Portland vase is of great interest for the quality of the relief, which is finely finished by hand (with undercutting) and appears to be polished. Unfortunately the vase is damaged but this allows us to see that the ceramic body is a slate-grey jasper, and has been given a dip of a vivid mid-blue akin to the colour of the copy given to the British Museum in 1802 by John Wedgwood. However, a greyer, inky-blue tone indicates the transparent parts of the original cameo glass, not the bright blue layer of the ground. The subtle application of a pale wash of inky blue deceives the eye. The experimental nature of this vase is underlined by the various darker additions of blackish blue on the upper surface of the relief.

The vase might possibly have been made in April 1791 when there was a temporary shortage of the black clay.[1] Otherwise it should probably be dated earlier than Wedgwood's first successful black vase, which was fired in 1790. It had been Wedgwood's original intention to make various editions for 'various purses'. Early blue copies have sometimes been considered a cheaper alternative but the Deutsher blue copy[2] is as highly finished as any. It is an experimental and most carefully considered variant.

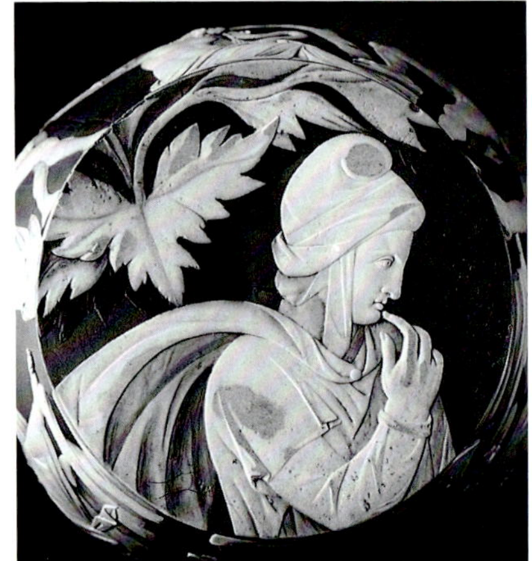

NOTES

1   For the shortage see Reilly (1989) vol. I, pp. 677–79.
2   The vase is listed by Dawson (1984) p. 150. It was sold by Sotheby's, London, 20 November 1979.

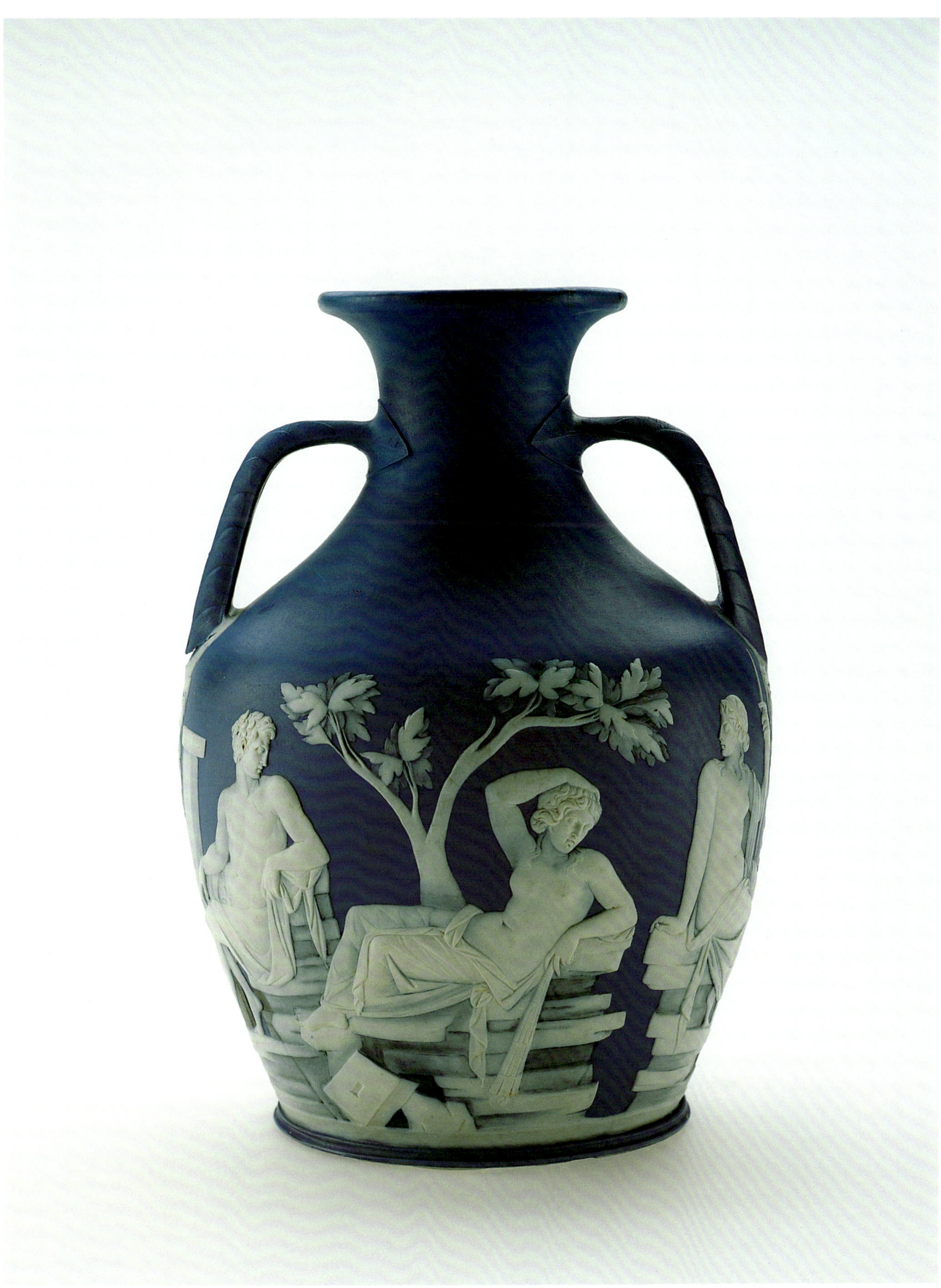

32 *Five intaglio gems*
18th century

stoneware (basalt)

Clockwise from top left:

Hygia (Hygeia)
2.2 x 1.8 x 0.3 cm
Impressed mark: WEDGWOOD / 279

Escalapius (Asclepius)
3.4 x 2.4 x 0.3 cm
Impressed mark: WEDGWOOD / 309

Sabina
2.1 x 1.8 x 0.3 cm
Impressed mark: WEDGWOOD / 19

A victory holding a pike
2.5 x 2.0 x 0.3 cm
Impressed mark: WEDGWOOD / 7

Alexander
2.6 x 2.2 x 0.3 cm
Impressed mark: WEDGWOOD / 140
(Note: *Alexander* appears as no. 240 in the
1779 *Catalogue*.)

Presented through The Art Foundation of
Victoria by Mrs Norma Deutsher, Governor
1994   (D26-1994)

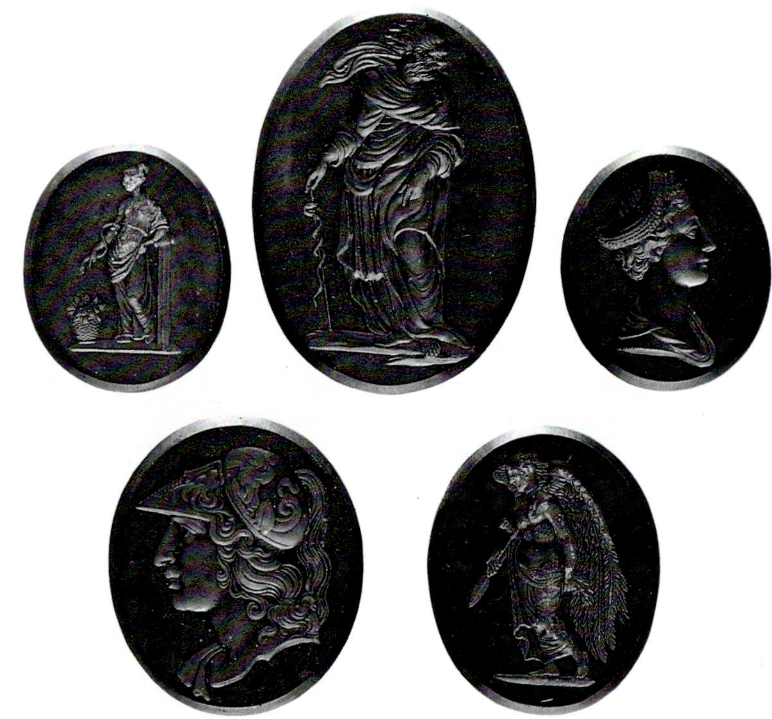

These oval gems bear the designs in the
negative (intaglio), for use as seals. The
subjects are all listed in the 1779
Catalogue. It describes the intaglios as 'far
above all other Imitations or Copies of
antique Gems, yet no Article, in the
whole Extent of the fine Arts has ever
been offered to the public at so
moderate a Price'. Large collections of
antique gems were formed by the
aristocracy and imitations in glass paste
and in plaster supplied the less wealthy.
Wedgwood developed his basalt copies
for a growing market.

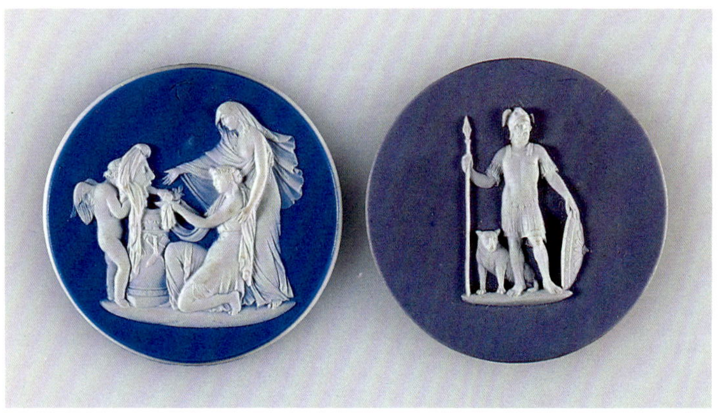

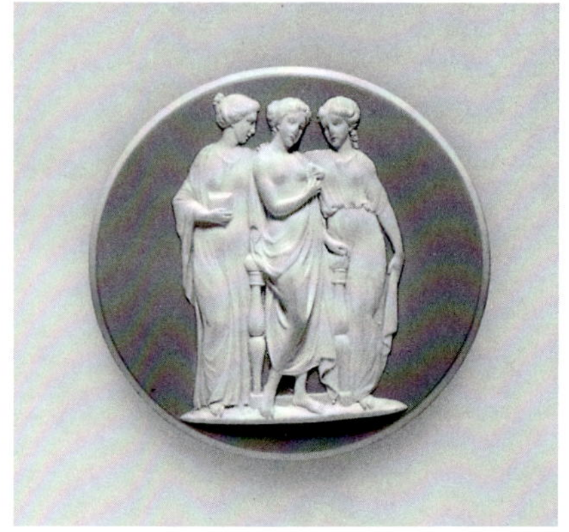

33 *Three cameos* 18th century

*Sacrifice with two women
and a putto wearing a mask*
stoneware (blue jasper dip)
5.1 x 5.1 cm
Impressed mark: WEDGWOOD

Mars
stoneware (lilac jasper dip)
5.1 x 5.1 cm
Impressed mark: WEDGWOOD

Three Graces
stoneware (blue jasper dip)
5.4 x 5.4 cm
Impressed mark: (in a curve) WEDGWOOD

Presented through The Art Foundation of
Victoria by Mrs Norma Deutsher, Governor
1994   (D31-1994, D33-1994, D32-1994,)

Cameos were widely collected as fine
examples of antique design. The figure of
Mars is after a statue from Brescia. It was
published by Montfaucon (vol. VI,
Supplement, p. 94 and pl. XXXVI of
vol. I), who identified the animal which
accompanies the god of war as a wolf, a
relatively unusual attribute.

Wedgwood's cameos could also be
used for everyday purposes, and these
circular cameos were sometimes
mounted as buttons.

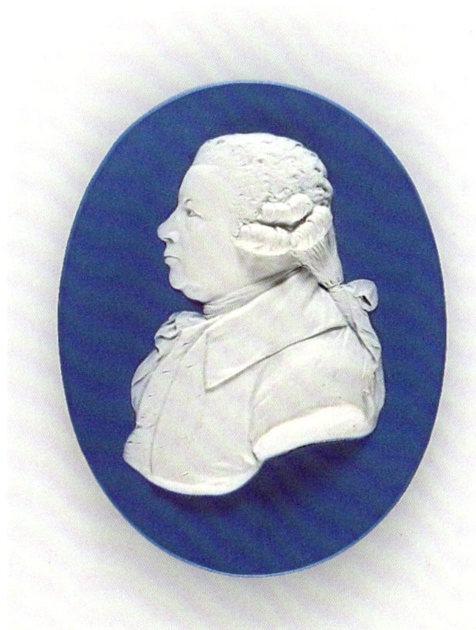

34 *Medallion — Dr Ralph Griffiths (1720–1803)* c. 1790

stoneware (blue jasper dip on slate-blue)
8.0 x 6.2 x 0.9 cm
Impressed mark: WEDGWOOD
Felton Bequest 1940   (4735-3)

Dr Ralph Griffiths (1720–1803), LL.D. Philadelphia, was the founder of the Monthly Review and brother of Thomas Griffiths, who sought out 'Cherokee clay',[1] a china clay, in South Carolina for Josiah I Wedgwood. In London he lived near Thomas Bentley at Turnham Green.

The medallion has a lapis-blue jasper dip on a solid slate-blue jasper ground. Large holes have been introduced at the back of the relief area, to prevent distortion in firing.

NOTE

1   Josiah I experimented with diverse clays, and kept a quantity of Virginian 'Cherokee clay', to which he referred in his patents, primarily to confound his imitators.

35 *Medallion — Josiah Wedgwood (1730–1795)* 1790s

Model by William Hackwood (d. 1839) 1782
stoneware (blue jasper dip)
10.2 x 8.1 x 1.6 cm
Impressed mark: WEDGWOOD
Incised on truncation of bust: WH
Purchased 1868   (236-1)

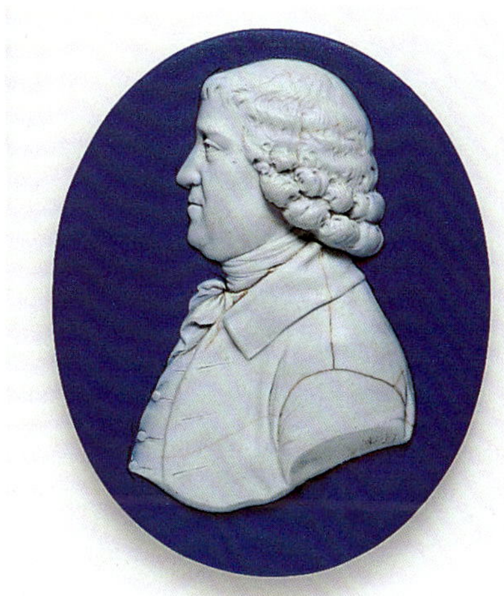

This medallion of the first Josiah Wedgwood,[1] in lapis-blue jasper dip, is a rare example of a work signed by the modeller. William Hackwood had been with Wedgwood since 1769, and it seems right that they should be associated in this way, although Wedgwood actively discouraged his modellers from signing their work.

In a letter to Bentley, 20 September 1769, Wedgwood described the young Hackwood as 'An Ingenious Boy. He has modelled at nights in his way for three years past, has never had the least instruction, which circumstances considered he does things amazingly … I have hired him for five years.' The self-taught modeller reached a standard comparable with John Flaxman and stayed with the company until 1832, well after the death of Josiah I in 1795.

At the time of purchase (1868), the Gallery's medallion was recorded as being made of Sydney clay, and this information was inscribed on the reverse by its previous owner, William Story. If this is so, it contains some of the clay which was sent to Wedgwood in 1788 by Captain Phillip via Sir Joseph Banks, President of the Royal Society, and was used for the *Sydney Cove* or *Hope* medallion.[2] In 1860 Story had written an essay on agriculture in Victoria[3] in which he mentioned that in Staffordshire he had known 'the late Mr Wedgwood, of Maer, son of the great potter' and that Josiah II (1769–1843) had given him the medallion portrait of his father together with the information that it was made from 'the Botany Bay clay'. Josiah II had emphasised Josiah I's high regard for the Sydney clay which was a potential import from the Colony.

The claim that the medallion contains some Sydney clay is corroborated by its unusual technical characteristics. The white relief of the medallion has been lightly tinted with blue, presumably in order to mask a fairly coarse body like the white body which is visible at the edges. There is some crazing[4] in the relief, with signs of old repair, perhaps indicative of problems with a new batch of clay.

NOTES

1   Reilly & Savage (1973) p. 334, medallion type c. Another signed example is illustrated there. The medallion is pierced with two large holes at the back to facilitate firing, and has a hand-cut groove for suspension.

2   For Wedgwood, clay from New South Wales and the *Sydney Cove* medallion see Smith (1978).

3   Story (1861) pp. 114–15. I am much indebted to Terence Lane for this reference.

4   Cf. crazing of the British Museum's portrait medallion of Sir John Jervis, c. 1798 (see Dawson 1984, fig. 57) and one of Edward Bourne, c. 1795 (Reilly 1989, vol. I, fig. 803c).

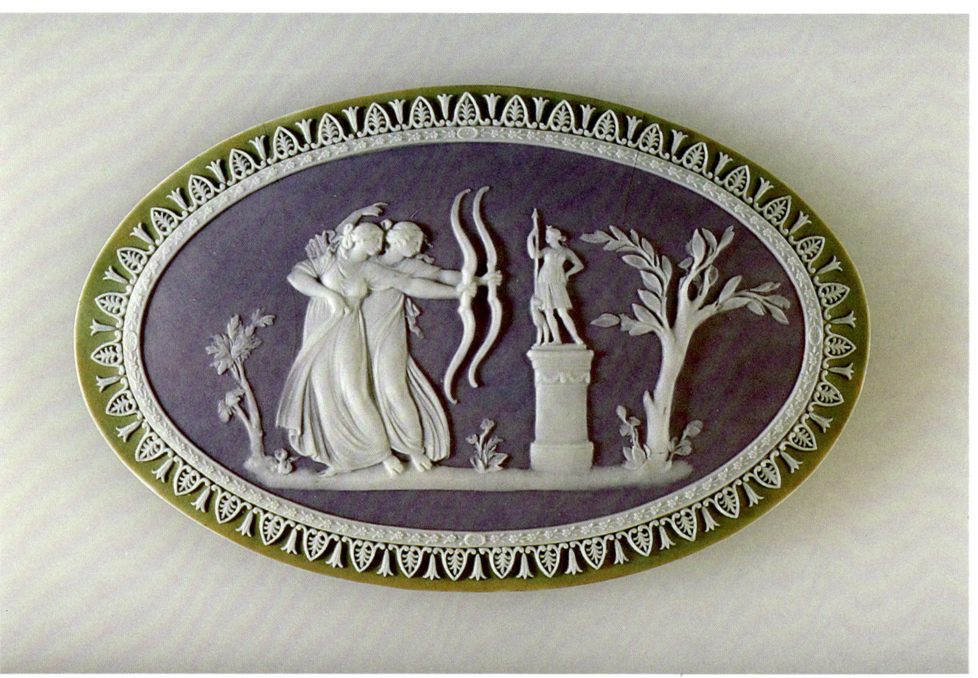

36A Medallion — Votaries of Diana c. 1790

stoneware (lilac jasper dip with green)
6.5 x 10.3 x 1.1 cm
Impressed mark: WEDGWOOD; and circle
K. and N. Deutsher collection

The domed oval medallion shows two young women practising archery near an image of Diana the Huntress. The domed shape is unusual and might suggest a later date. No source for this particularly graceful design is known.

36B Medallion — Friendship consoling Affliction c. 1790

stoneware (lilac jasper dip with blue)
7.7 x 11.9 x .06 cm
Impressed mark: WEDGWOOD; and circle
K. and N. Deutsher collection

The design derives from an ancient relief now in the Louvre, which shows a woman washing the feet of a bride who is weeping. (Illustrated by Montfaucon, vol. III, second part, pl. CXXXII, the original was once in the Palazzo Albani in Rome.) It was adapted for Wedgwood by Lady Templetown, who is acknowledged as its designer in Wedgwood's *Catalogue* of 1787.

36C Medallion — Achilles dragging the body of Hector c. 1790

stoneware (lilac jasper dip with blue)
7.8 x 12.0 x 0.5 cm
Impressed mark: WEDGWOOD
K. and N. Deutsher collection

The design so exquisitely presented illustrates one of the most horrific episodes in the Homer's *Iliad*, where the Greek hero Achilles drags the body of the vanquished enemy around the walls of Troy. A larger version of the design, facing the opposite direction, was modelled by Camillo Pacetti (1758–1826), working for Wedgwood in Rome from 1787 to about 1789. It was one of six reliefs after the antique Luna marble disc presented to the Capitoline Museum by Pope Benedict XIV not long before.[1]

This style of medallion was used for inlaying in furniture, and a similarly shaped medallion was used on a famous Broadwood harpsichord of 1796, designed by Sheraton and presented to the Queen of Spain.[2]

Notes
1   Reilly (1989) vol. I, pp. 599-601.
2   It is now at the Heritage Foundation, Deerfield, Massachusetts. See Reilly (1989) vol. II, figs. 845–46; Kelly (1965) figs 65, 66.

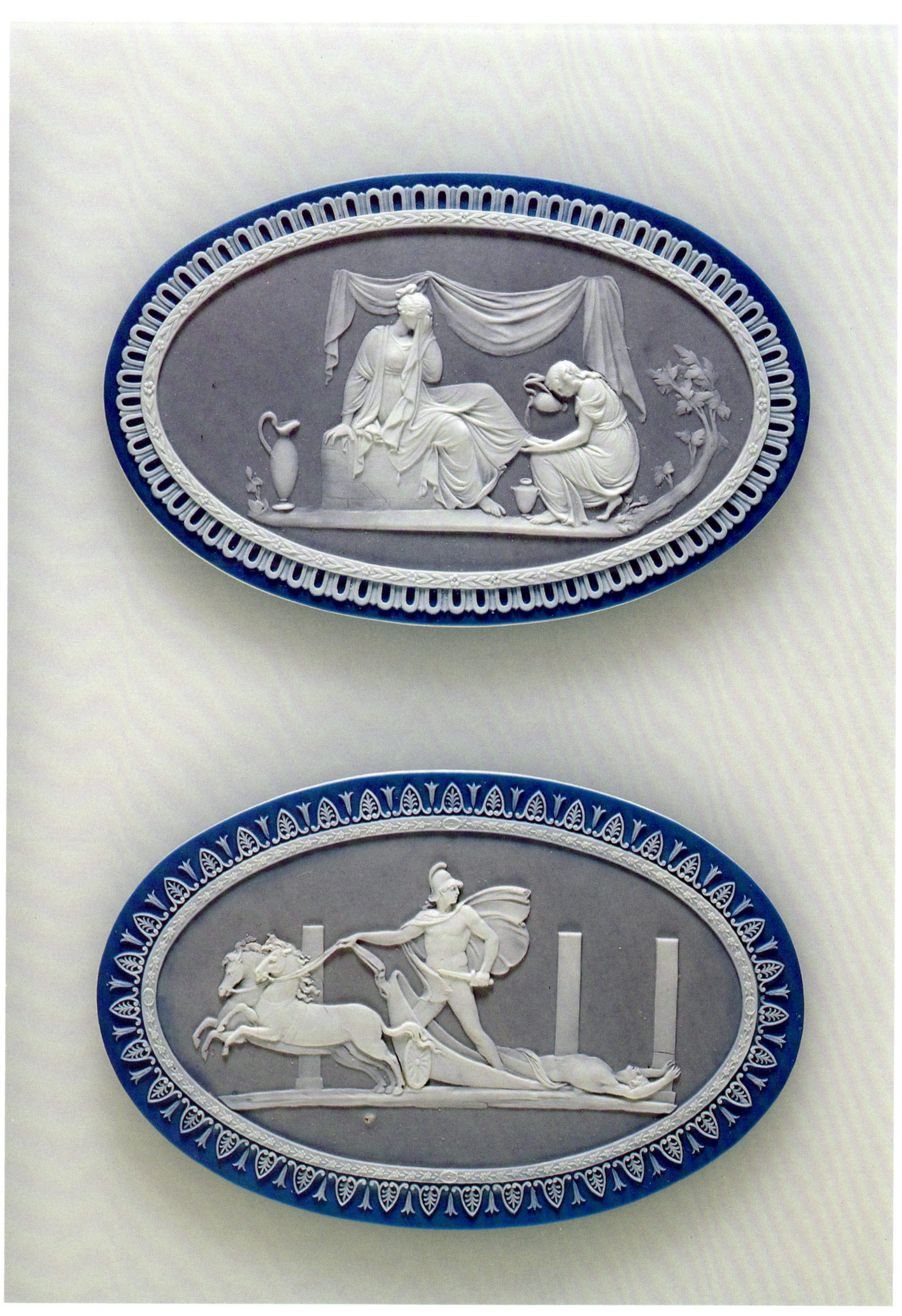

37 *Perfume bottle* c. 1790

stoneware (blue jasper)
15.0 x 6.5 x 2.5 cm
Unmarked
K. and N. Deutsher collection

The navette-shaped perfume bottle is
decorated on both sides with 'Domestic
employments' by Lady Templetown. It
has a lapidary polished edge (that is, it
has been polished using the techniques of
the gem engraver), and is typical of the
gem-like small items produced in the
18th century.

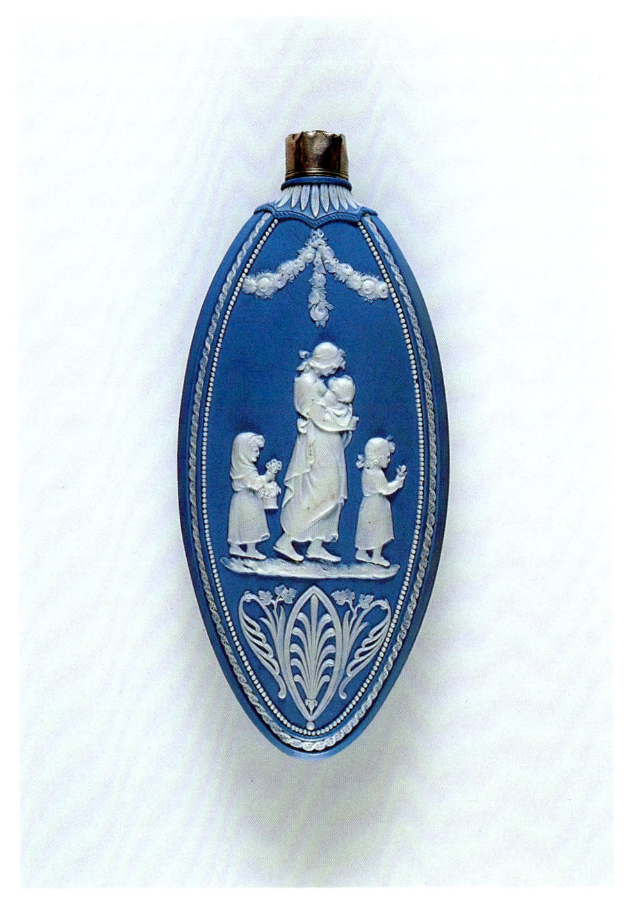

38 *Snuff box* c. 1790

stoneware (blue jasper) plaque, ivory,
gold, glass
4.8 x 8.7 x 1.9 cm (plaque 2.0 x 5.4 cm
within frame)
Purchased 1917   (186-3)

The lapis-blue and white relief
showing a group of gods (a
composite scene with Neptune
and Aesculapius) is set as a gem
under glass in the lid of an ivory
box trimmed with an escutcheon,
hinges and line borders of gold.
Wedgwood cameos were
mounted 'under Crystal' for
protection and to enhance the
precious effect.

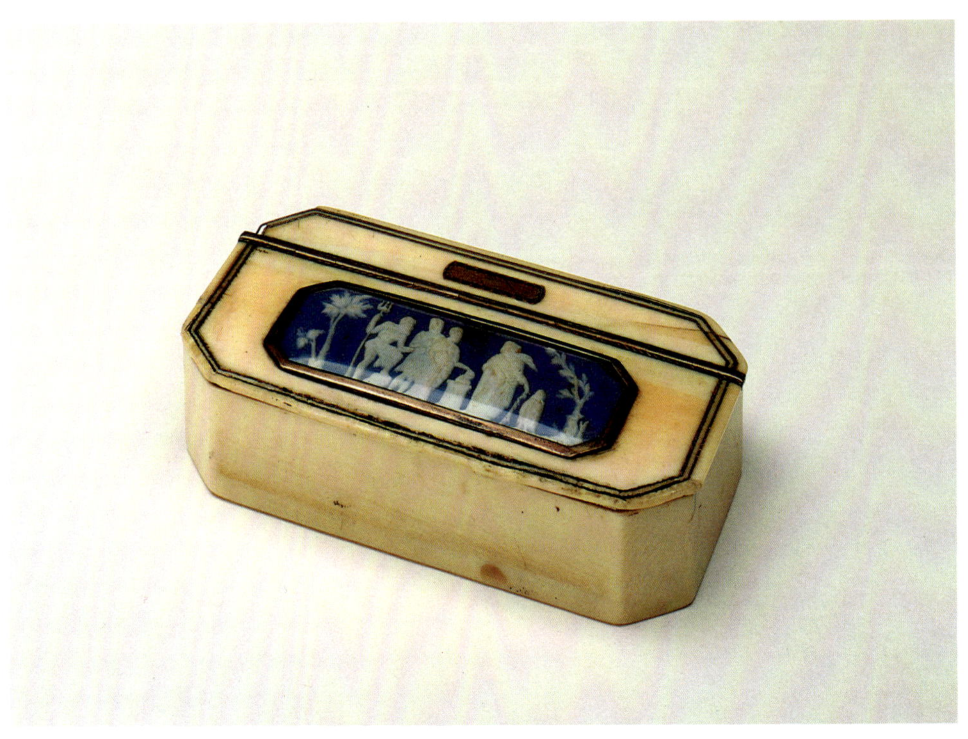

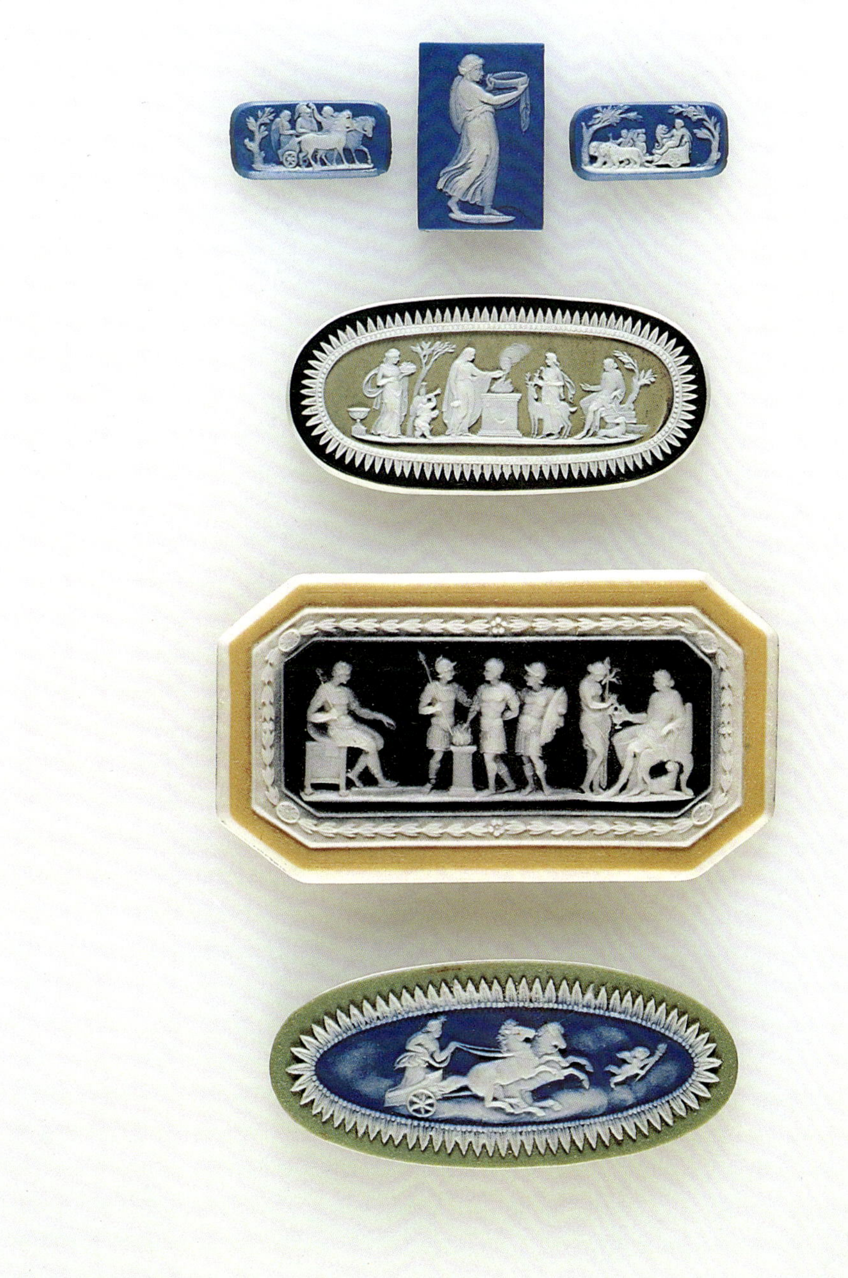

39 Six cameos
18th–19th centuries

The Vestal Tuccia with her sieve
18th/19th century
stoneware (blue jasper dip)
2.3 x 2.0 cm Unmarked

Pair of chariot scenes
19th century
stoneware (blue jasper)
1.0 x 2.0 cm Unmarked

Sacrificial scene
18th century
stoneware (green jasper dip with black)
2.5 x 5.2 cm
Impressed mark: WEDGWOOD; and circle

Sacrificial scene
19th century
stoneware (black jasper dip with yellow)
3.8 x 6.9 cm
Impressed mark: WEDGWOOD

Aurora
18th/19th century
stoneware (blue jasper dip with green)
2.5 x 5.7 cm
Impressed mark: WEDGWOOD

Presented through The Art Foundation of
Victoria by Mrs Norma Deutsher, Governor
1994   (D28-1994; D27A,B-1994; D35-1994;
D36-1994; D34-1994)

This group of small cameos shows the
type of production most adapted for
jewellery and other small personal items
(note the lapidary polished edges of the
oval sacrificial scene and the two small
chariot scenes). The small rectangular
blue jasper gem with the Vestal Virgin
Tuccia, who demonstrated her chastity by
carrying water in a sieve, appears in the
Catalogue of 1787. The design may be
compared with Montfaucon, vol. VI
(Supplement) and pl. XXIII of vol. I.

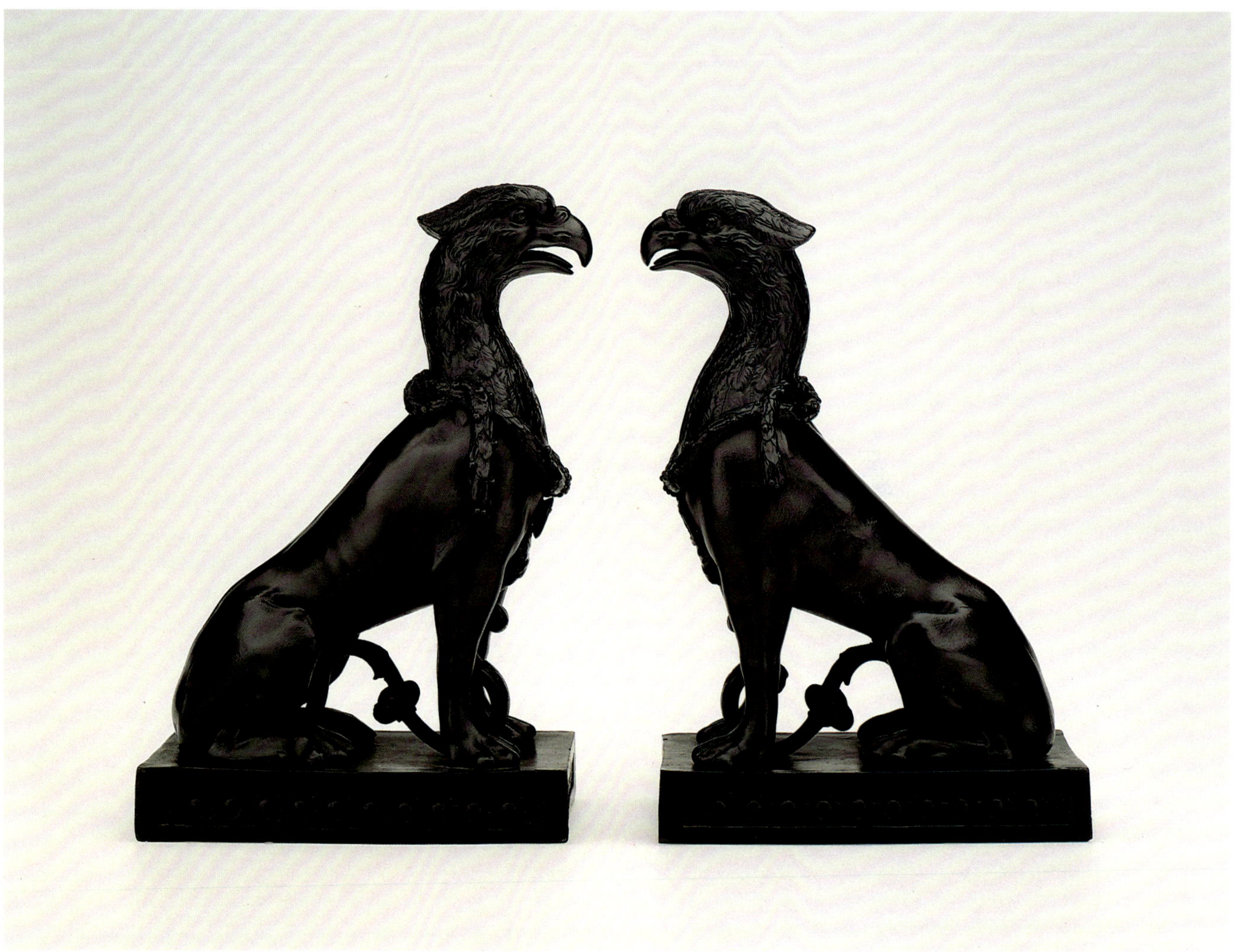

40 *Pair of griffins* 1780–1800

stoneware (basalt)
A 24.6 x 16.8 x 9.3 cm
B 24.4 x 16.8 x 9.4 cm
Impressed mark on A: WEDGWOOD
K. and N. Deutsher collection

Each figure is in the form of a seated monster with its ornate tail scrolling beneath the body, its neck draped with festoons from which is suspended a medallion. One shows a centaur with a child (Charon and Achilles), the other Hercules and the Nemean lion. As early as November 1771 Wedgwood was preparing to make candlesticks using the griffin design. He may have obtained this from the architect Sir William Chambers (1726–96), who published a similar design in *A Treatise on Civil Architecture*, 1792. The wooden block mould for the griffin is preserved in the Wedgwood Museum, Barlaston.

41 *Pie dish* 1795–1805

stoneware (caneware)
6.8 x 21.2 x 14.7 cm
Impressed mark: WEDGWOOD / G
Presented through The Art Foundation of
Victoria by Mr Keith M. Deutsher, Founder
Benefactor 1993   (D15-1993)

The shallow oval dish and cover are
modelled in imitation of a pie, with a pie-
crust edge to the dish and pastry-style
lattice-work on the cover, and with a
finial in the form of a nut.

Imitation pies do not appear in
Wedgwood invoices until 1795. However,
the idea seems to have come in 1786
from Wedgwood's friend, the author
Richard Lovell Edgworth, who requested
'oval baking dishes in the form of raised
paste pies … made of cane-coloured
ware'.[1] On 24 December 1786,
Wedgwood wrote to him: 'I made a clay
pye and shewed it to my children as the
best judges, but they not knowing what it
was intended for, convinced me at once
that it was wrong, and I have not yet
made another essay.'[2] Dishes in imitation
of pastry were in great demand during
the flour shortages of the 1790s and
later.

NOTES

1   Buten (1980) p. 178. Richard Lovell
    Edgworth (1744–1817) was married to
    a grand-daughter of John Philip Elers,
    famous early potter of fine red stone-
    ware in Staffordshire.
2   Finer & Savage (1965) p. 302.

42 *Conceit* 1795–1805

stoneware (caneware)
14.0 x 20.1 x 13.0 cm
Impressed mark: WEDGWOOD / G
K. and N. Deutsher collection

The model of a dessert cake of
biscuits and decorative icing is made
in caneware with white jasper, its top
moulded with a trophy including a
lyre, set within a wreath. *Trompe-l'oeil*
models made a witty and amusing
table decoration, and were
particularly serviceable when real
cakes and pies were not available.
The uneven texture of the biscuits is
skilfully rendered.

43 *Covered jar*
   c. 1795

stoneware (lilac jasper dip with
green)
20.2 x 13.8 x 13.8 cm
Impressed mark:
WEDGWOOD / S
Incised with three radiating
dashes
Presented through The Art
Foundation of Victoria by Mr
Keith M. Deutsher, Founder
Benefactor 1993
(D12-1993)

The cylindrical container is
in the form of a circular
domed building, with six
equally spaced Corinthian
pilasters, set on a stepped
base. The surface is
decorated in lilac wash with
white relief and with a dice
pattern of sage-green
quatrefoils in white squares.
The cover, possibly a later
replacment, has a taper-holder finial.

The architectural form recalls the
monument of Lysicrates, otherwise
known as the Lanthorn of Demosthenes.
A copy of the ancient building was
constructed by the architect and
antiquarian James 'Athenian' Stuart at
Shugborough, Staffordshire, for Lord

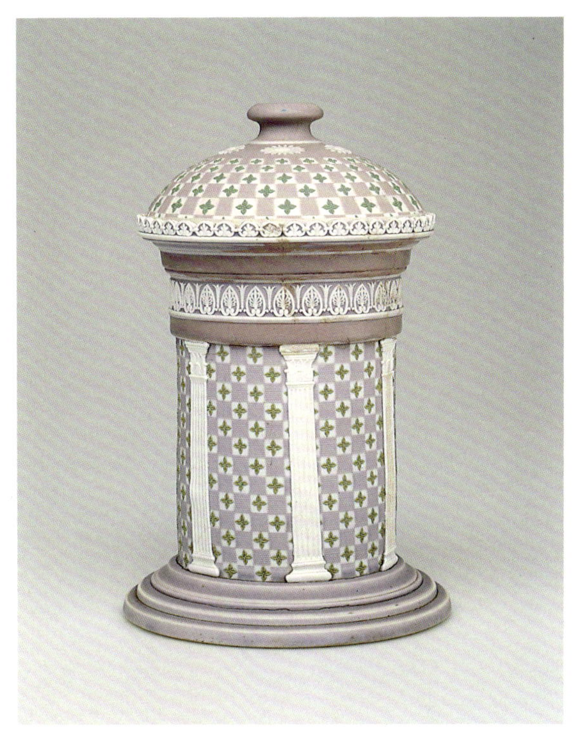

Anson. It was well known to Josiah I
Wedgwood, who offered to make the
bowl for the tripod Stuart proposed to
put on top of the dome.

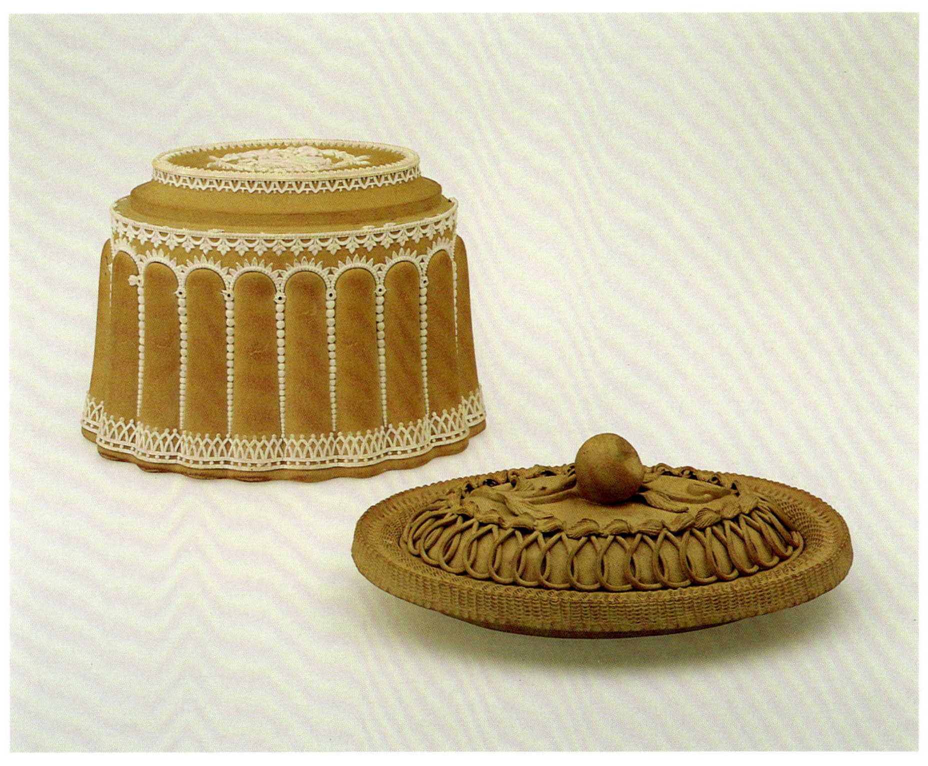

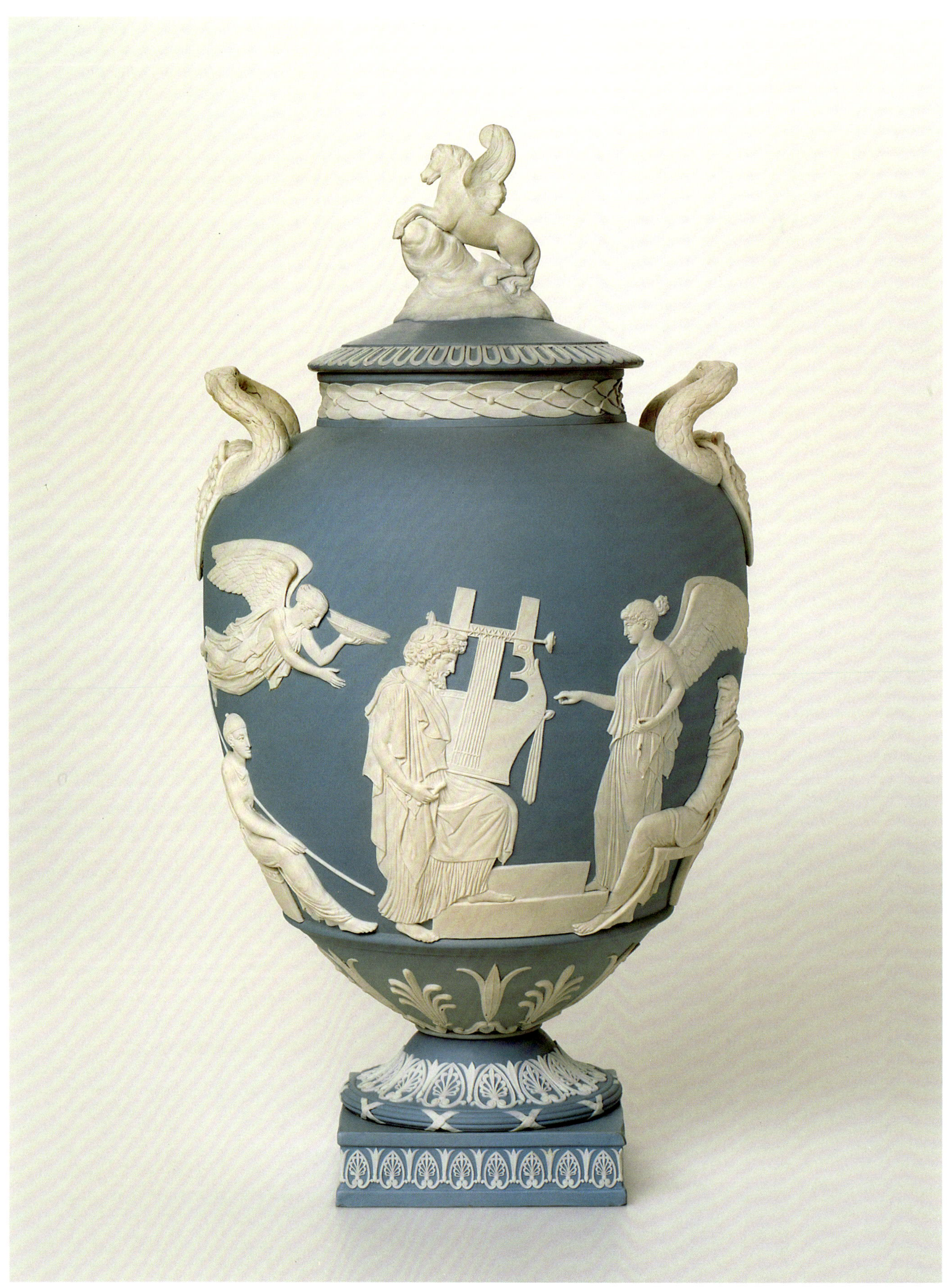

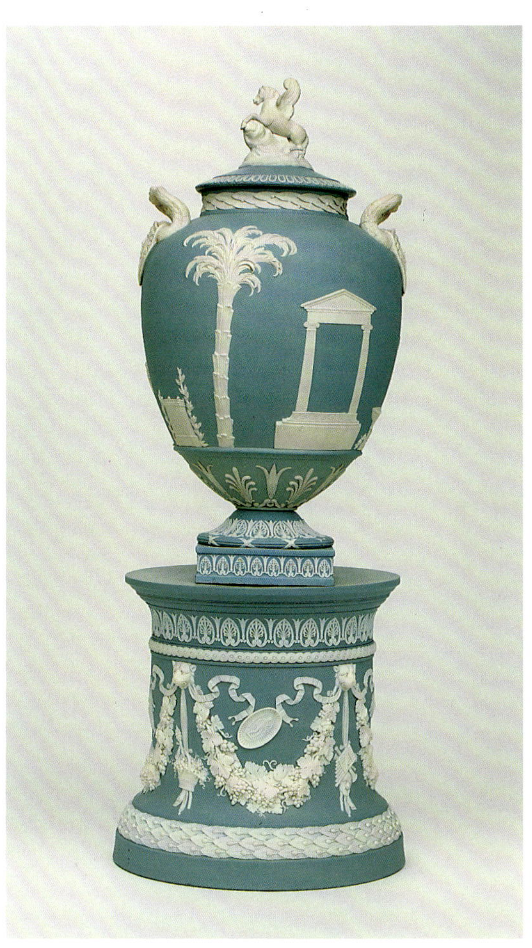

44 *Homer vase* c. 1800

stoneware (blue jasper)
vase 48.1 x 25.5 x 25.3 cm
Impressed mark: WEDGWOOD / 2 2
pedestal 27.7 x 27.8 x 27.6 cm
Impressed mark: WEDGWOOD
Presented through The Art Foundation of
Victoria by Mr Keith M. Deutsher, Founder
Benefactor 1993   (D14-1993)

The vase, with a finial in the form of the
winged horse Pegasus, has serpent-
shaped handles emerging from Medusa
heads, and a socle foot set on a square
base. The relief decoration shows the
Apotheosis of Homer, modelled by John
Flaxman after a Greek red-figured bell-
krater in the collection of Sir William
Hamilton, illustrated in d'Hancarville, vol.
III, p. 31. The reverse of the vase shows a
palm tree (cf. Montfaucon, vol. III, pl.
XXXVI) and a small classical monument
with a triangular pediment.[1] The drum-
shaped pedestal, decorated with festoons
and trophies, is based on the form of a
classical urn (cf. Montfaucon, vol. V, pl.
XXVIII).

D'Hancarville describes the subject as Homer, a priest of the Muses, about to sing for another poet, possibly Hesiod, with the *Iliad* personified seated and holding a lance while its 'genius' mounts the altar and the 'genius' of the *Odyssey* hovers in the air (vol. III, p. 210). (The ancient artist depicted a player of the lyre or *kithara* mounting the podium to sing in a contest. The interpretation by D'Hancarville would not be accepted now.)

The *Apotheosis of Homer* relief first appeared as a plaque in the Wedgwood & Bentley *Catalogue* of 1779. The young John Flaxman interpreted the red and black of d'Hancarville's illustration to make a low relief design of great elegance.

The technique of Greek vase painting emphasised the silhouette, and this aspect of the antique was newly prized by the rising generation of Neoclassical artists, who were seeking purity and simplicity. In the opinion of the influential art historian of the period, J. J. Winckelmann, the essence of ancient Greek art was 'noble simplicity and calm grandeur'. Flaxman, always the master of harmonious composition, made full use of the expressive and well-spaced silhouette effect and enriched the internal detail of the figures with his gentle but taut modelling in low relief. Subtle adjustments of the details of figure style have made the design recognisably Flaxman's own. His only intervention in the content of the composition was the provision of a simple seat for the left-hand figure, which would otherwise appear to float against the background, and he, or the factory, has mistakenly made the *kithara* with a solid piece behind the strings.

In 1786 Josiah Wedgwood sent Sir William Hamilton a jasper plaque with the design after his antique vase, thoughtfully presented in a silk-lined mahogany box, and intended to publicise his wares abroad. Hamilton duly replied: 'I never saw a bas-relief executed in the true simple antique style half so well.' In the same year Wedgwood presented a blue jasper *Homer vase* to the British Museum, calling it 'the finest and most perfect I have ever made'.

1   On Wedgwood's *Homer vase* in the British Museum there is a statue of Athena framed by its columns. Dawson (1984) supposes that a vase lacking the figure of Athena would date from after the death of Josiah I, when the mould may have been lost.

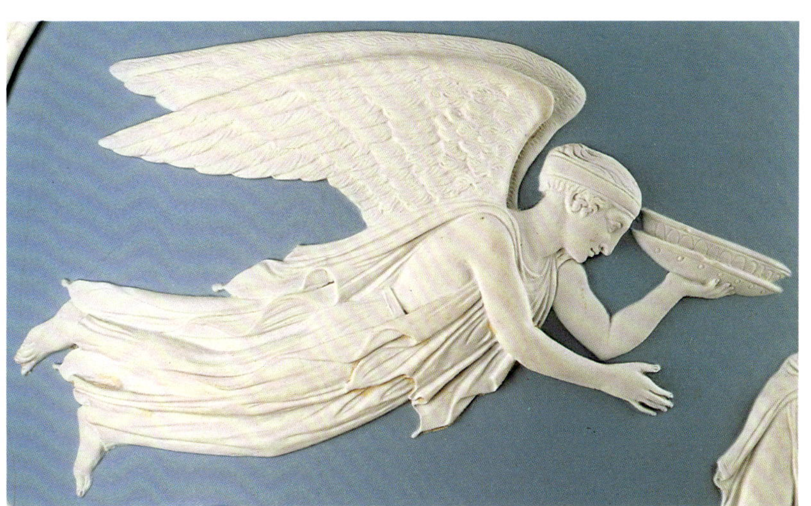

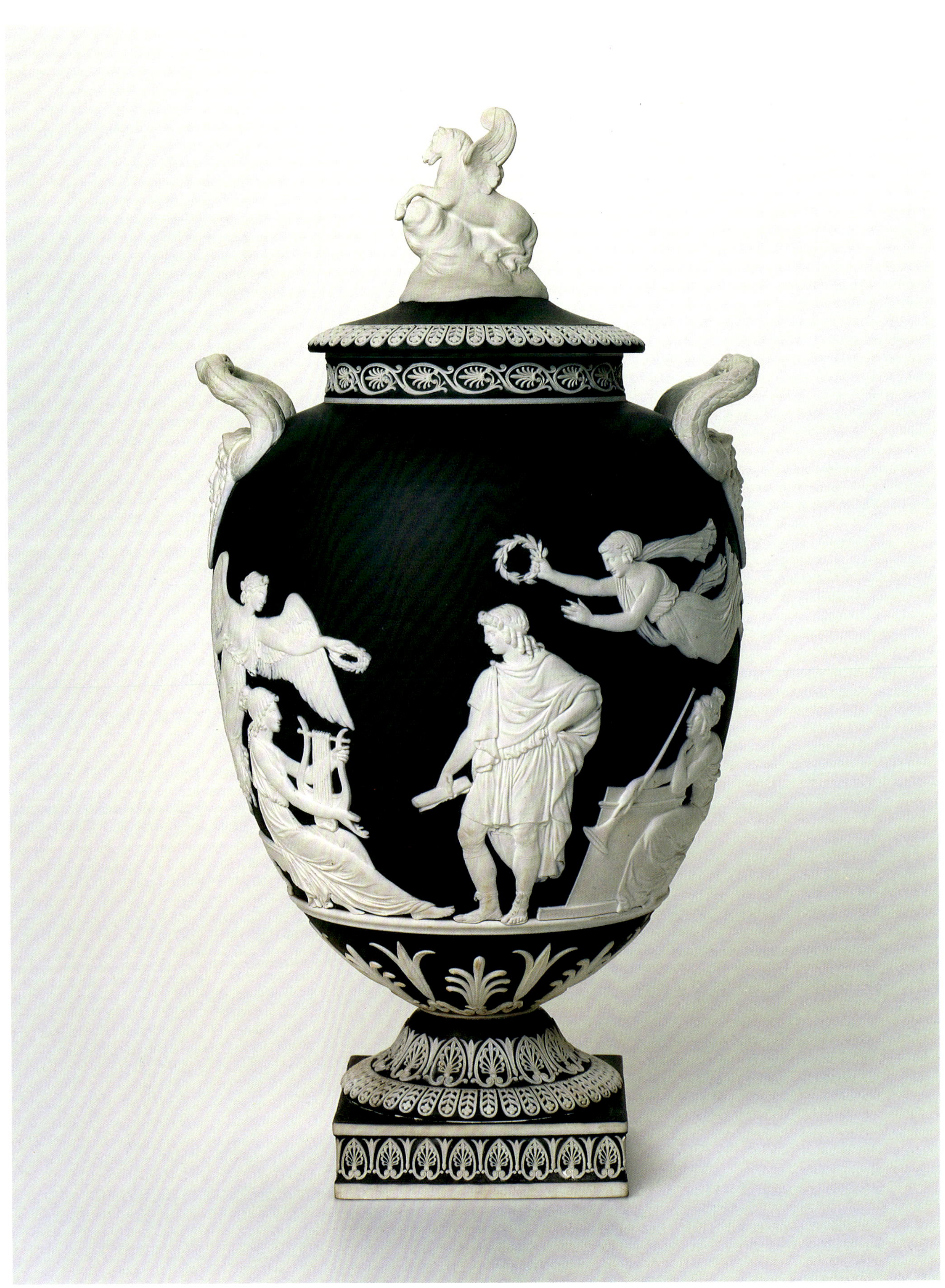

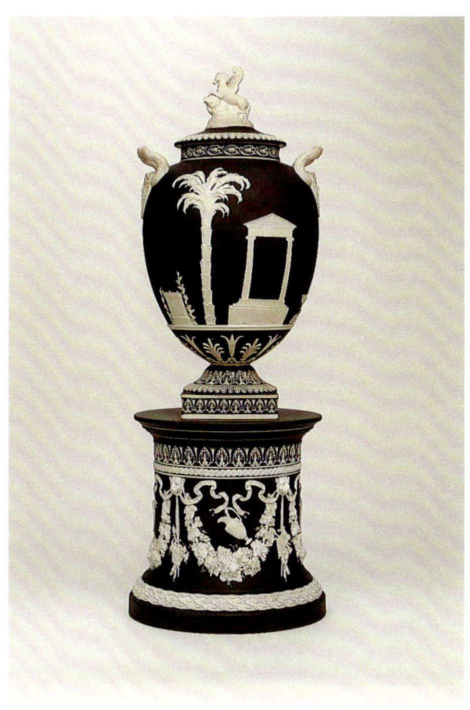

45 *Virgil vase* 19th century

stoneware (black jasper dip)
vase 51.0 x 27.0 x 26.0
pedestal 29.0 x 28.8 x 28.8 cm
Impressed mark: WEDGWOOD
Incised mark in the form of a dash
Presented through The Art Foundation of
Victoria by Mrs Norma Deutsher, Governor
1994   (D21-1994)

This vase, of similar shape to the
preceding *Homer* vase, differs in the
substitution of a diagonal anthemion
border for the stiff leaves at the mouth of
the latter, and in the decorative borders
of the foot and lid. The relief of the
Apotheosis of Virgil was modelled as a
companion piece to the *Homer* relief. A
tablet with this subject first appeared in
the *Catalogue* of 1787.

The young poet stands, with a scroll
in his hand, between a woman with a lyre
and another with a trumpet. Behind her
appear war-like attributes, a helmet and a
spear. Above, two winged Victory figures
offer crowns, and the one on the left also
holds the panpipes symbolic of rustic
music.

No classical source for this design is
known. It seems the subject was invented
as a parallel to the *Homer* as interpreted
by d'Hancarville: while the earlier poet
appears with figures d'Hancarville
believed to represent his *Iliad* and
Odyssey, Virgil is celebrated on the one
hand for his pastoral poetry (the

panpipes) and on the other for his
famous epic, the *Aeneid,* which begins
'I sing of arms and the man'.

The relief here is also attributed to
John Flaxman. Its softer and more
decorative style is perhaps a
conscious reflection of the contrast
between the austere style of the
ancient Greek poet and the
mellifluous and almost romantic
qualities of his Roman imitator.

Extant examples of the design all
seem to date from the 19th century.
The present vase is finely finished,
but lacks the degree of undercutting
seen on the *Homer vase.* The drum
pedestal is of similar design, but of
slightly different proportions.

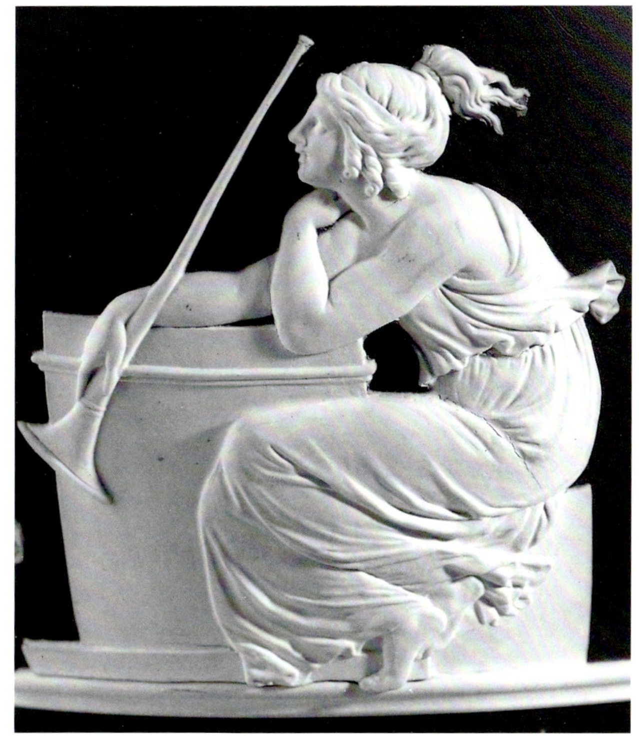

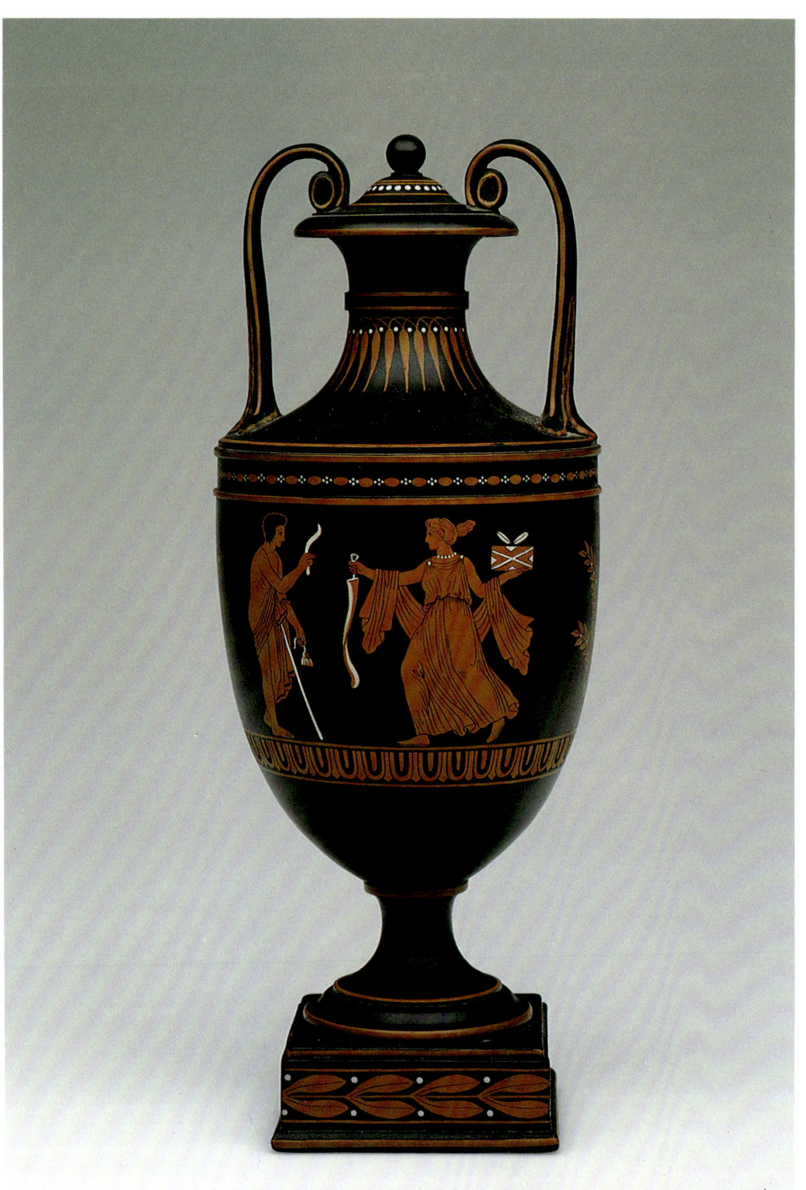

The 'encaustic' decoration of this small plate or stand consists of a rich border with scrolling leaves and flowers, delicately executed in white pigment which is raised somewhat on the surface, and a central design of radiating lines and stylised husks, the details in matt red.

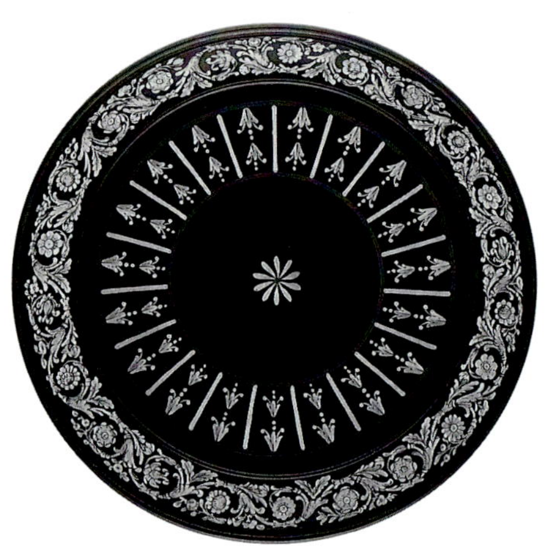

46 *Vase* c. 1815

stoneware (basalt)
27.8 x 11.1 x 11.0 cm
Impressed mark: WEDGWOOD
Presented through The Art Foundation of Victoria by Mr Keith M. Deutsher, Founder Benefactor 1993   (D17-1993)

The shield-shaped covered vase has high handles terminating in small paterae at the mouth and is set on a waisted socle and square base. It is decorated in 'encaustic' technique,[1] in imitation of ancient red-figure style, with a draped youth with a staff and a strigil (the scraper used in classical antiquity to remove oil from an athlete's skin when bathing) and with a woman bearing a fillet or headband of the sort offered as prizes to athletes. The figures are set between trees above a border of 'egg and dart' pattern and there is a myrtle wreath on the square base.

The male figure is derived from d'Hancarville (vol. I, pl. 74) where the object held by the youth is similarly represented as a flower (in the Greek original it would have been a small pot for perfumed oil).

Wedgwood's 'encaustic' technique of decoration in matt colours was developed at the very beginning of the Wedgwood and Bentley partnership for the express purpose of imitating ancient vase-painting 'without the Defect of a varnished or glassy surface. An object earnestly desired by Persons of critical Taste in all Ages'.[2]

NOTES

1   The term 'encaustic' actually refers to painting in wax, as described by the ancient author Pliny.
2   *Catalogue,* 1779, Class IX.

48 *Vase (bough-pot)*
c. 1815

stoneware (basalt)
27.3 x 21.3 x 21.3 cm
Presented through The Art
Foundation of Victoria by Mr
Keith M. Deutsher, Founder
Benefactor 1993   (D16-1993)

The campana-shaped vase
with a flat pierced cover has
polychrome enamel
decoration in the Chinese
famille rose style consisting of
scattered flowers and foliage.
The early 19th century saw an
eclectic mix of stylistic
influences from east and west.
This bright and informal
oriental decoration was
combined with European
shapes in basalt, white
stoneware, drabware and *rosso
antico* (see below).

49 *Vase* c. 1815

stoneware (rosso antico)
29.8 x 22.7 x 21.5 cm
Impressed mark: WEDGWOOD / N
Presented through The Art Foundation of
Victoria by Mrs Norma Deutsher, Governor
1992   (D10-1992)

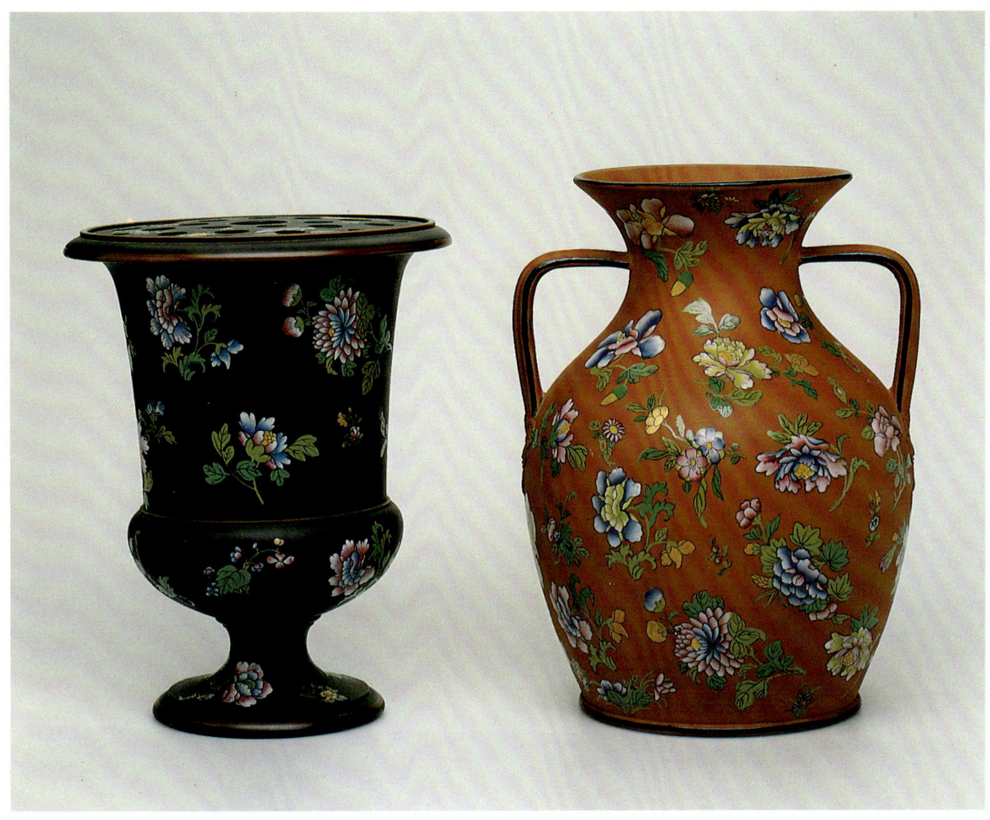

This vase is shaped like the *Portland vase,*
with two handles terminating in crisply
modelled satyr masks and is decorated in
coloured enamels with scattered flowers
in the Chinese *famille* rose style.

The red stoneware or *rosso antico*
(antique red) body was a refined version
of the Staffordshire red ware used in the
early 18th century to imitate Chinese Yi-
Hsing wares. Josiah Wedgwood adapted
it for use on classical forms about 1776
at the instigation of Thomas Bentley.
However he did not like its close
association with ordinary teawares, and
the body was not much used until after
his death in 1795. The Italian term was
originally used for a highly prized type of
statuary marble used in ancient Rome.

50 *Saucer* c. 1810

earthenware (drabware)
2.6 x 13.9 x 13.9 cm
Impressed mark: WEDGWOOD
Presented by John H. Connell 1914   (1178-2)

The neutral-coloured body of the deep
saucer forms a particularly effective
background for the colours of the
flowers and butterfly in Chinese *famille
rose* style. A small bird is sitting on a
flowering branch.

The drab-colour, containing nickel,
was developed in the 18th century but,
like the rosso antico, was not much used
before 1800. It was made both as
a stoneware body and in earthenware,
where it required glazing to seal the
surface against liquids.

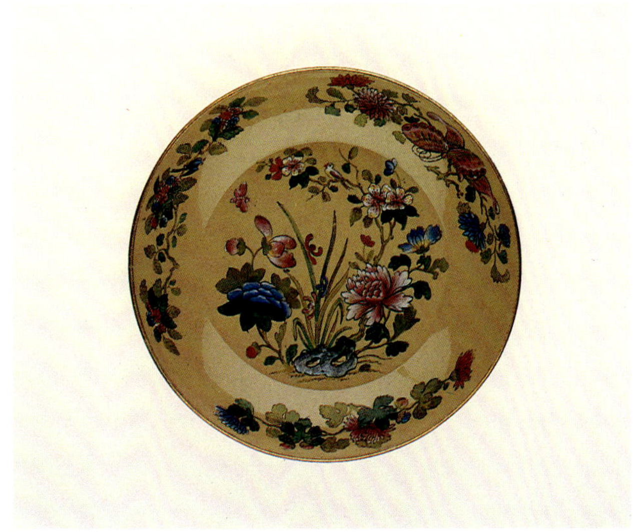

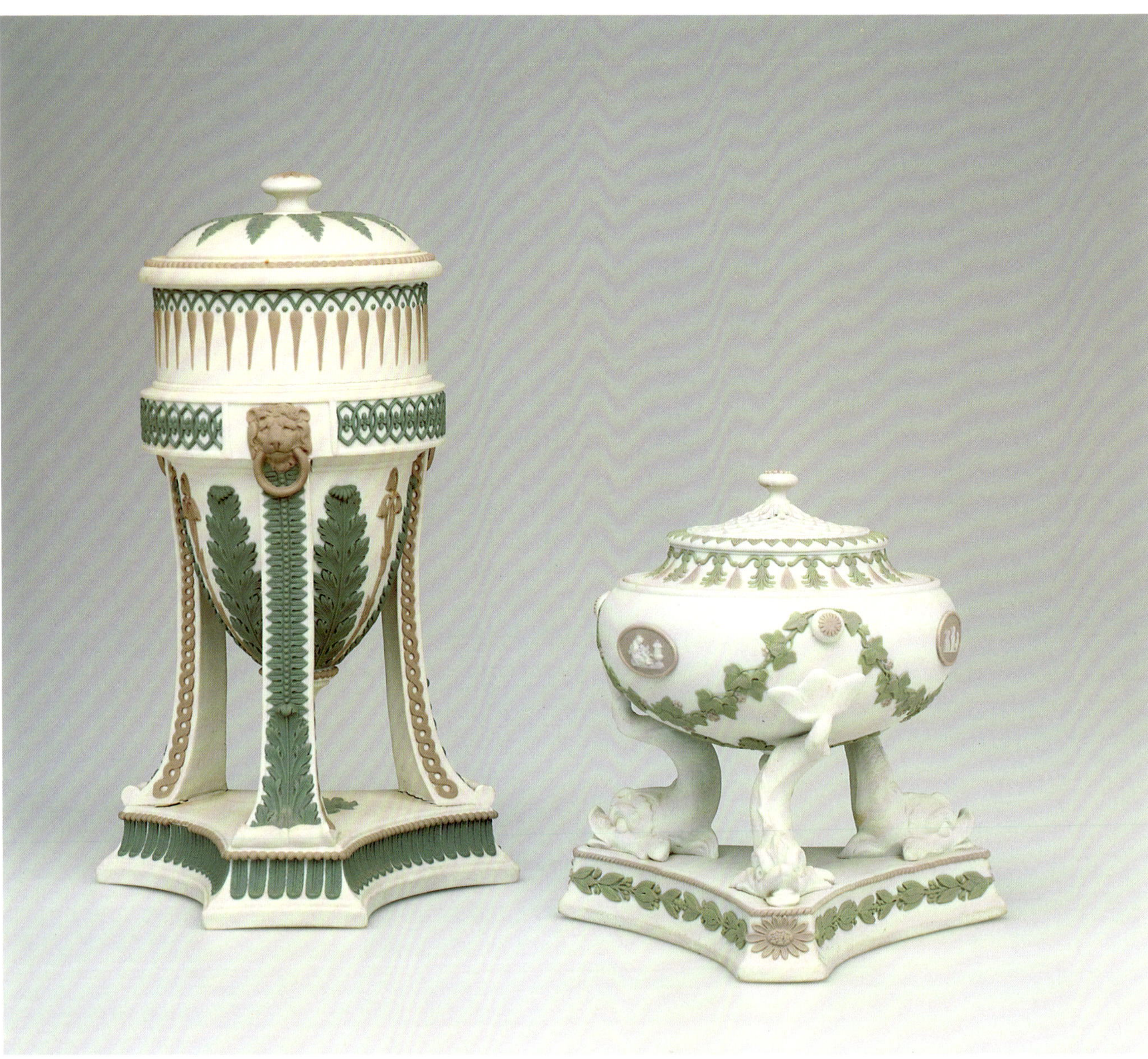

51 *Tripod incense burner*
c. 1820

stoneware (white jasper with green and lilac)
12.9 x 11.1 x 12.7 cm
Impressed mark: WEDGWOOD
Presented through The Art Foundation of
Victoria by Mrs Norma Deutsher, Governor
1993   (D23-1993)

The pastille burner is supported by three
dolphins on a shaped triangular base, the
white body with relief decoration in
green and lilac. It has a delicately pierced
cover, and three small holes in the base
help the flow of air.[1] Incense burners
were widely used in the early 19th
century (see cat. nos 57, 60). They are
generally small decorative pieces but very
large ones were ordered for large rooms.

NOTE

1   A letter from Tom Byerley 1808, pointing
    out the necessity of putting in the holes, is
    quoted in Roberts (1984) p. 45, cat. no.
    N3.

52 *Tripod vase* c. 1820

stoneware (white jasper with green and 'cafe
au lait')
21.5 x 12.9 x 11.2 cm
Impressed mark: WEDGWOOD / J
Presented through The Art Foundation of
Victoria by Mrs Norma Deutsher, Governor
1993   (D24-1993)

The covered vase, which emulates an
ancient tripod, is raised on three legs,
each terminating with a lion mask at the
body. The legs are decorated with
acanthus and guilloche borders and set
on a three-sided base. The body has
coloured relief decoration consisting of
an 'antique dart' border at the mouth
and vertical acanthus leaves alternating
with harebells below.

53 *Plate* c. 1810

stoneware (caneware)
18.5 x 18.5 x 1.7 cm
Impressed mark: WEDGWOOD
K. and N. Deutsher collection

The light-coloured caneware plate has a border of prunus blossom and bamboo in white relief. The pattern was known as 'Chinese ornaments'.

The cane colour is a 'dry body' (unglazed material), developed by 1770 from local marl (calcium-rich earth), but not perfected until the 1780s. It formed a vitreous material of matt appearance, with a colour which varied from tan to yellow–buff. Caneware was used for a wide variety of forms, and in particular imitated the natural colour of cane or bamboo which was in demand for the *chinoiserie* style. This was to reach a new climax with the decoration of the Brighton Pavilion, commissioned and built in Hindu–Chinese style 1815–21.

54 *Jug* c. 1815

stoneware (caneware)
11.9 x 13.1 x 10.3 cm
Impressed mark: WEDGWOOD; and comma mark
K. and N. Deutsher collection

The small jug has an overall pattern of basket-weave, with a band of herringbone pattern below the rim, and is painted with lines of dark-blue enamel at the mouth and handle. The precise and complex basket-weave pattern has been achieved by engine-turning,[1] while the herringbone is a roulette pattern (see note to cat. no. 21). The handle, moulded with a different type of basket-weave,

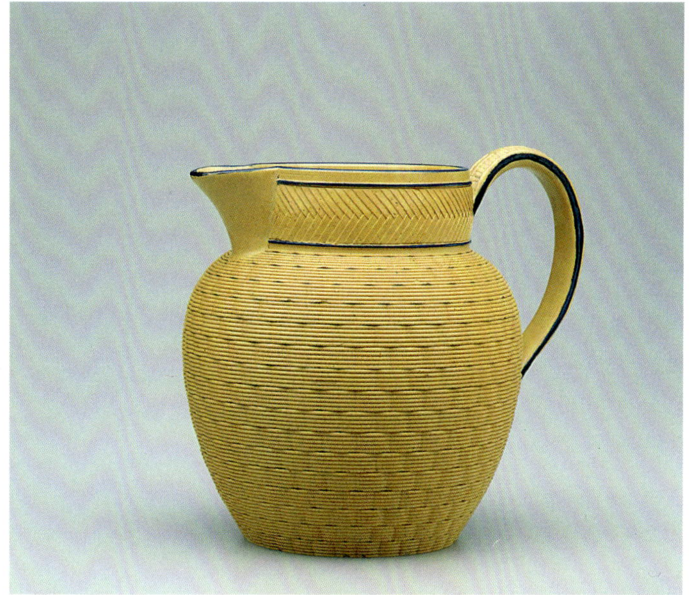

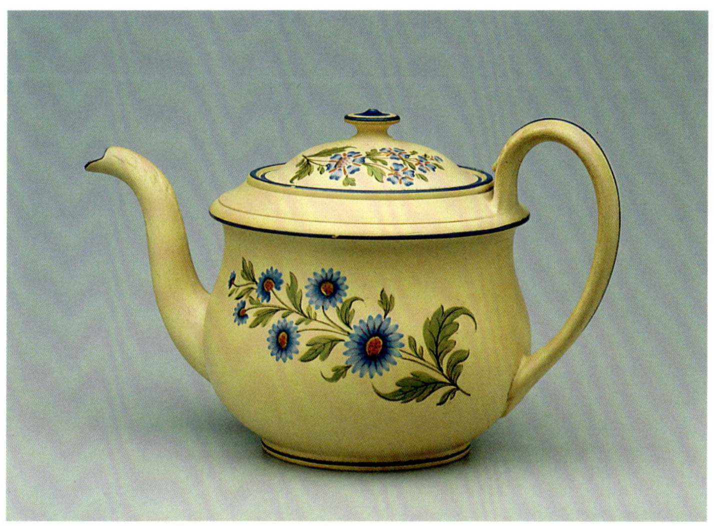

may also have been made using a roulette to create a flat, decorated strip which could be bent into shape.

NOTE

1   The turning of the basket pattern is described in detail in Adeney (1989) p. 108.

55 *Breakfast setting* c. 1815

stoneware (caneware)
Impressed mark on each piece:
WEDGWOOD
tray 2.7 x 40.0 x 33.0 cm
teapot 11.0 x 18.1 x 10.6 cm
K. and N. Deutsher collection

The oval tray, teapot (illustrated), creamer, sugar box, two cups and saucers, and bowl are made in light-coloured caneware decorated with

scattered sprays of flowers in bright enamel colours, and with blue line edges. The interiors are glazed to prevent staining. The flowers, which are painted simply and without three-dimensional effects, the angular shapes of the cups, and the teapot with its flat top and high handle represent the changing taste of the early 19th century.

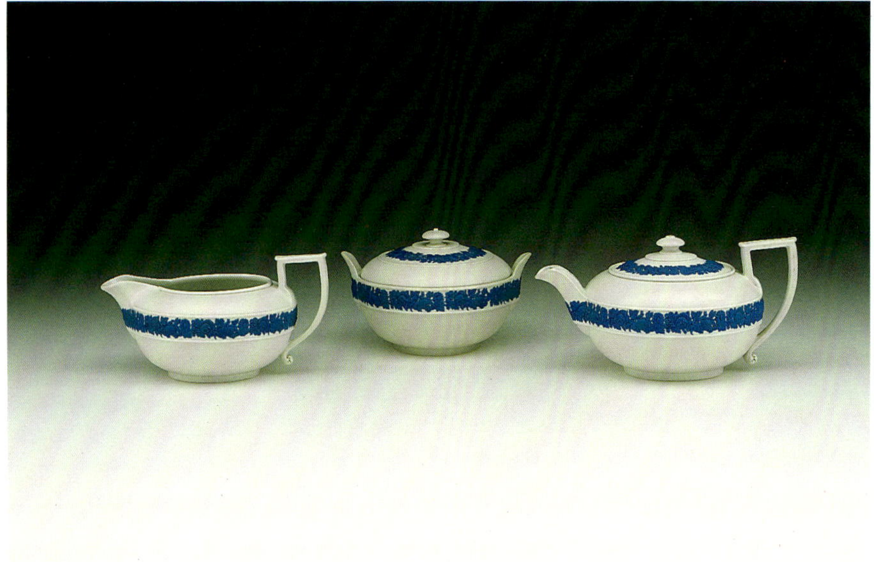

of dark-blue jasper dip below the rim, on which there are classical scenes interspersed with anthemion motifs. The base is in the same jasper dip, decorated with horizontal palmettes. (Note the whiteness of the jasper reliefs in comparison with the colour of the exposed stoneware body of the vessel.) There is a pierced lid to hold a floral arrangment. This style of vase was also fitted with a solid lid below the pierced one, and this was used as a platform to burn perfume in the form of pastilles.

NOTE

1   The shape is probably from d'Hancarville (1766–67) vol. II, pl. 39.

56 *Teapot, sugar bowl and creamer* c. 1815

stoneware (smear-glaze)
teapot 8.4 x 16.6 x 11.5 cm
Impressed mark: WEDGWOOD / X; and circle
sugar bowl 8.0 x 13.1 x 11.0 cm
Impressed mark: WEDGWOOD / RK
creamer 7.7 x 14.6 x 10.4 cm
Impressed mark: WEDGWOOD; and circle
K. and N. Deutsher collection

The teapot, covered sugar bowl and cream jug are of squat globular shape (shape 43 of the *Catalogue* of 1817, engraved by William Blake) and banded with applied garlands of berries, leaves and flowers in deep-blue stoneware on the white stoneware body.

The characteristic thin and slightly textured glaze is Wedgwood's smear glaze, first introduced for glazing white stoneware in 1815. A lead-based glaze[1] was applied in liquid form to the inside of the protective pottery boxes (saggars) in which the wares are placed to protect them from the flames, and it volatilised to glaze the wares.

NOTE

1   This glaze appears similar to salt-glaze, but in fact it contained lead (see Reilly 1989, vol. II, p. 484).

57 *Tazza vase* c. 1820

stoneware (blue jasper dip)
19.8 x 27.0 x 18.2 cm
Impressed mark: WEDGWOOD / RK
K. and N. Deutsher collection

The vase is in the form of a Greek drinking cup with high scrolling handles *(kantharos),*[1] decorated with a wide band

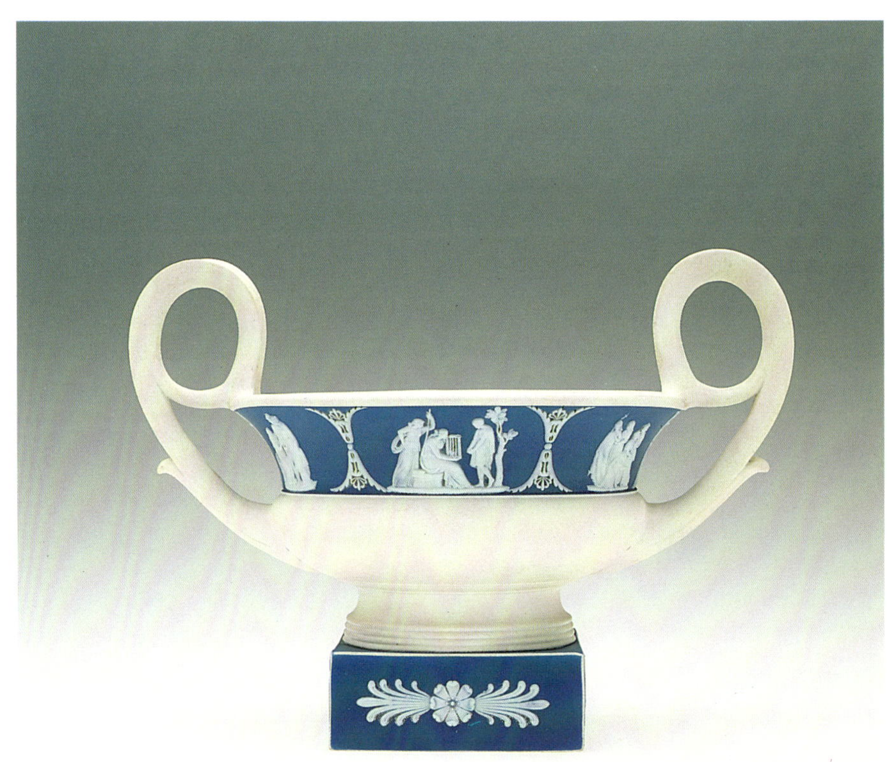

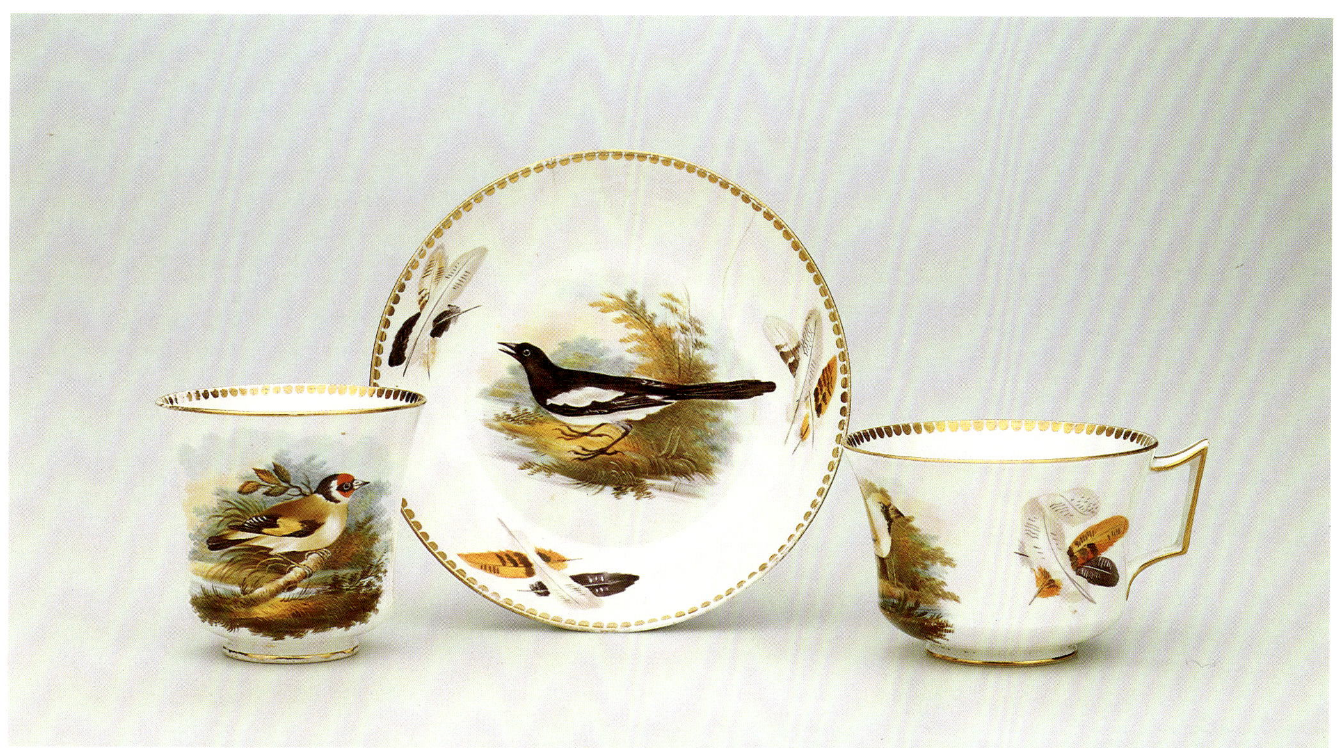

58 *Teacup, coffee cup and saucer* c. 1815

porcelain (bone china)
teacup 6.0 x 10.3 x 8.8 cm
coffee cup 7.1 x 9.2 x 7.6 cm
saucer 14.1 x 14.1 x 3.0 cm
Mark printed in red on each piece:
WEDGWOOD
Inscribed in purple on base of each piece
respectively: Grosbeak; Goldfinch; Magpie
K. and N. Deutsher collection

This trio was made in the first period of
Wedgwood's bone china production.
Each piece is decorated in colours with a
bird in a landscape and groups of
feathers, and has gilt dentil edges. This
attractive type of decoration (pattern no.
723), using typical motifs of the early
19th century, was the work of Aaron
Steele, who had previously been a
decorator in the 'encaustic' technique.

Josiah I Wedgwood had kept notes on
various porcelain recipes of his day,
including that of the Bow factory which
contained bone ash, William
Cookworthy's hard-paste porcelain
patent and the French hard-paste patent
of the Comte de Lauraguais of 1766.
However he preferred to persevere
along the surer course of his own
development of jasper. In the early 19th
century Josiah II Spode transformed the
ceramic industry with his bone china, and
Wedgwood's son Josiah II resolved to

follow. Experiments began about 1810,
and the first bone china was delivered in
June 1812. Dinner wares were not made
at this period; only teasets and a few
small ornamental pieces. Wedgwood's
early bone china was made with
Cornwall clay, Cornwall stone and bone
ash,[1] the last in considerably smaller
proportion than in modern recipes.
Josiah II Wedgwood decided to cease
bone china production in 1815 (though
replacements were ordered as late as
1831) and it was not resumed until 1868.

NOTE

1   Reilly (1989) vol. II, p. 593.

59 *Plate* c. 1815

porcelain (bone china)
21.5 x 21.5 x 2.8 cm
Mark printed in red: WEDGWOOD
K. and N. Deutsher collection

This plate, of lightly fluted shape, is
decorated with floral sprays printed in
black, and painted in enamel with green
leaves and pink flowers in various tones.
The pattern is no. 681, 'Botanical flowers
with gold diamond border, gold edge'.
The printed part of the design provided
some stipple shading as well as outline,
so that a less-skilled artisan could apply
the colours as simple washes and still
create a good effect.

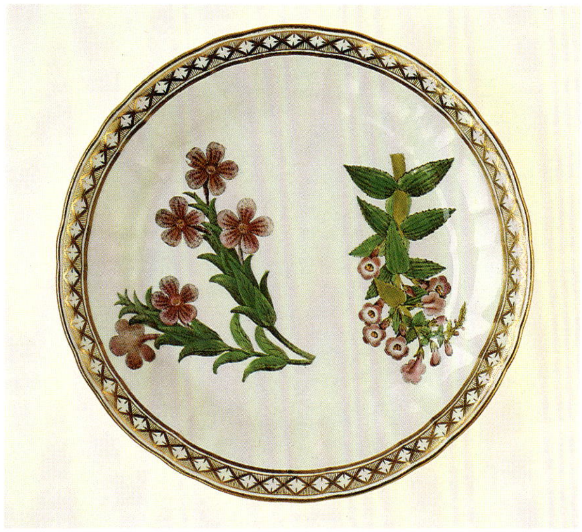

60 *Vase (pot-pourri)* c. 1820

earthenware (pearlware)
36.8 x 19.7 x 19.7 cm
Impressed mark: WEDGWOOD / ⊞
K. and N. Deutsher collection

The baluster-shaped vase has a pierced
cover and a solid inner lid, for use as
either a flower vase, a pot-pourri
container or a pastille burner (see cat.
no. 57). It has been lightly printed in
black and then painted in colours with
flowers and foliage beside a fence, in
chinoiserie style.

Pearlware was introduced in 1779, as
a whiter alternative to creamware. The
mark consisting of four squares is
associated with the period c. 1818–21.[1]

NOTE

1   Reilly (1989) vol. II, p. 652 (ills).

61 *Plate* c. 1830

stoneware (stone china)
23.7 x 23.7 x 2.3 cm
Mark printed in blue: WEDGWOOD'S /
STONE CHINA
Impressed mark: 5
K. and N. Deutsher collection

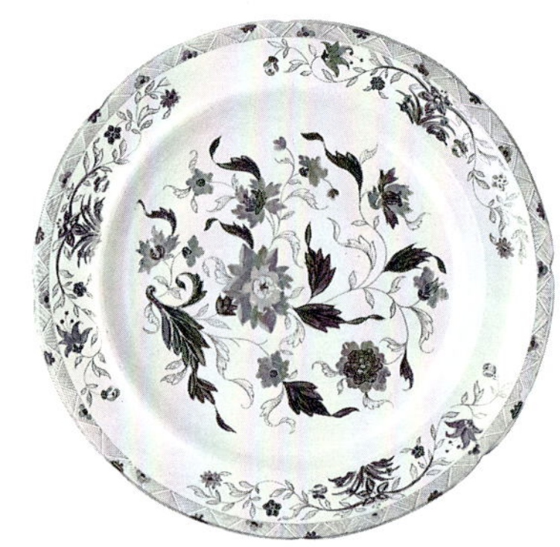

The floral 'Japan pattern' is printed in
iron red and ochre, and painted in deep
blue, iron red, yellow and gold. This sort
of bold floral design, which is loosely
derived from Japanese Imari wares of the
17th century, was much in demand in the
early 19th century. The stone china body
itself seems to have been developed
especially to imitate Oriental export
porcelain.

Wedgwood's stone china, produced
as a response to Spode's stone china and
Mason's popular ironstone, is a high-fired,
durable body of a greyish tint, made from
the basic ingredients of porcelain but not
transparent. It was used for only a limited
period, from 1820 to 1861.

62 *Canopic vase*
19th century

stoneware (green jasper dip)
26.2 x 13.3 x 13.3 cm
Impressed mark: WEDGWOOD; and semi-
circle
Presented through The Art Foundation of
Victoria by Mrs Norma Deutsher, Governor
1993   (D25-1993)

The vase is made in the manner of an
ancient Egyptian canopic vase, with a
cover in the form of man's head. The
body has hieroglyphs and signs of the
Zodiac in white relief. The canopic vase
shape was first introduced in the
Wedgwood & Bentley period, after a
design in Montfaucon (vol. II, pl.
CXXXII). The left-hand emblem on the
lower body is from his vol. II, pl. CXLI,
while the right-hand emblem and the
hieroglyphs seem to have been drawn
from the *Tabula Isiaca* (Isis tablet). The
latter is a mysterious Egyptian-style
bronze, actually a Hellenistic or Roman
work with nonsense hieroglyphs, which
was owned by Cardinal Bembo in the
early 16th century and was reproduced
in several publications, including
Montfaucon.

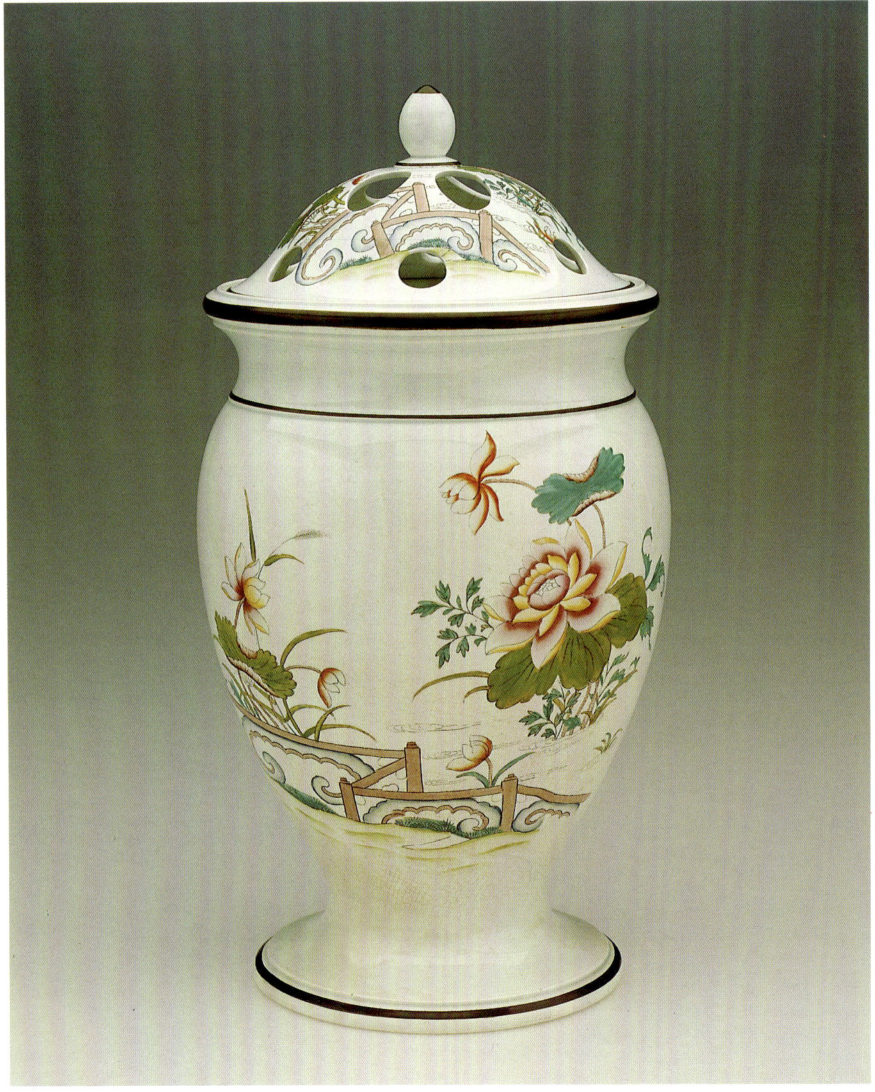

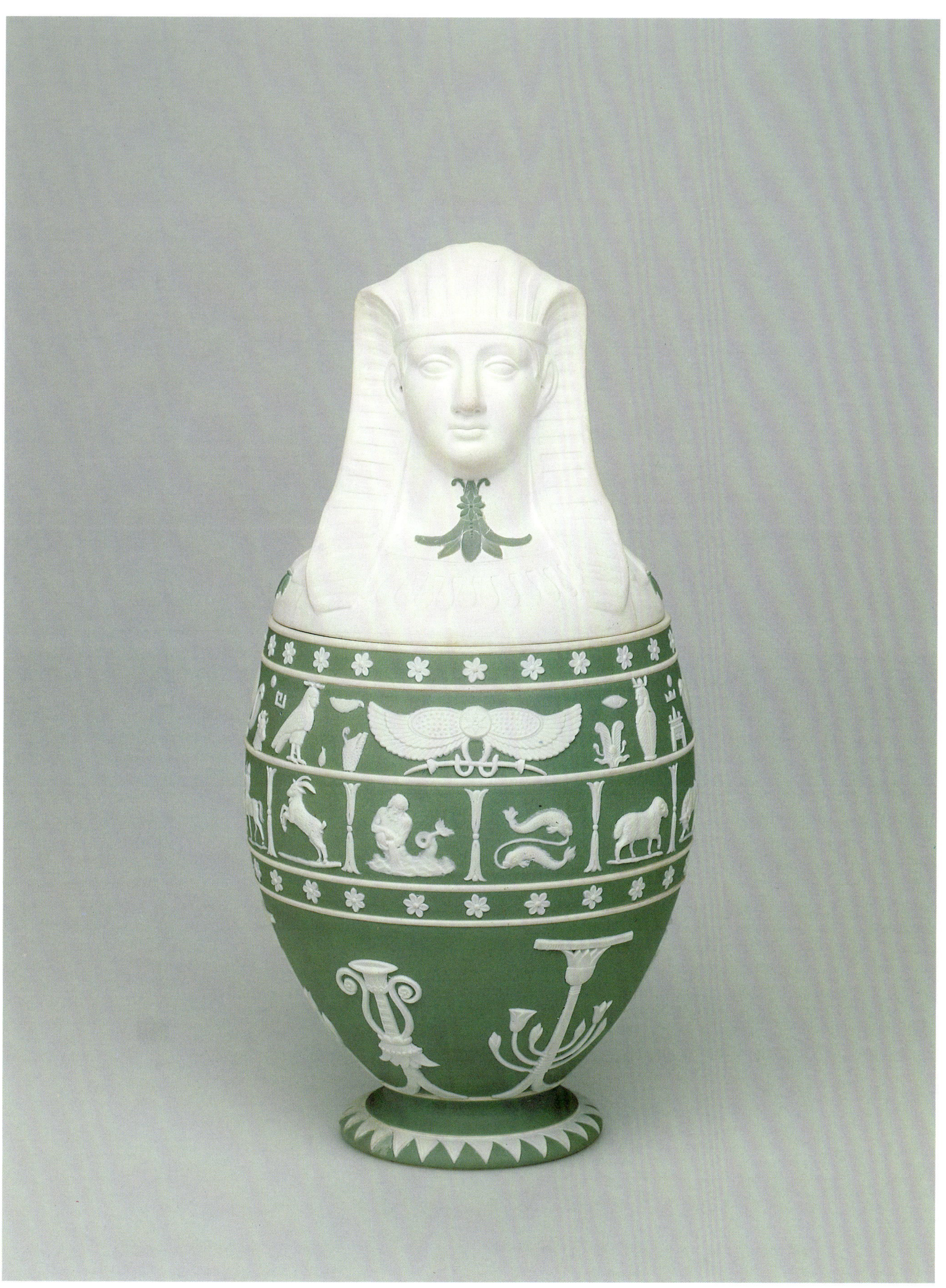

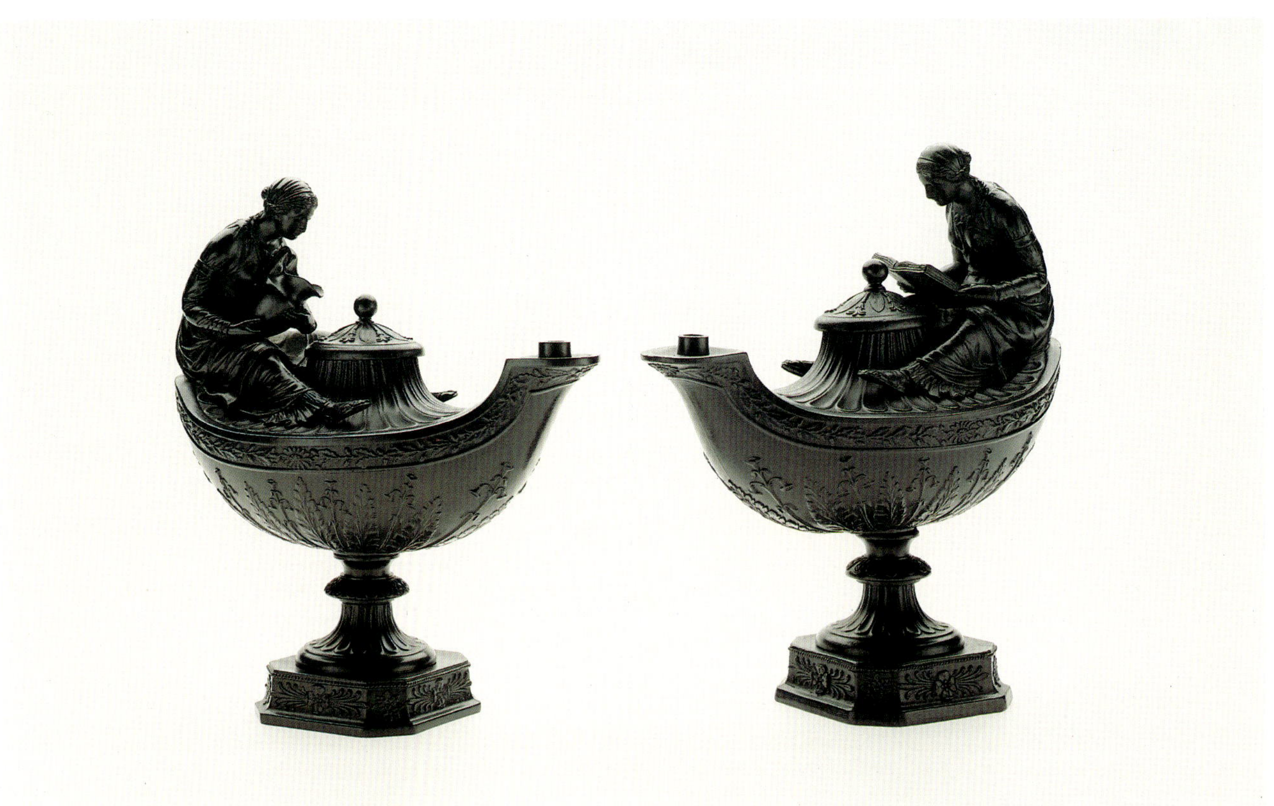

63 *Pair of 'Vestal' oil lamps*
c. 1860

stoneware (basalt)
figure reading 23.0 x 20.8 x 10.4 cm
Impressed mark: WEDGWOOD / C
figure with pitcher 21.8 x 20.3 x 10.2 cm
Impressed mark: WEDGWOOD / S
Presented through The Art Foundation of
Victoria by Mr Keith M. Deutsher, Founder
Benefactor 1993   (D18-1993)

The boat-shaped lamps resemble antique
oil lamps consisting of a covered
container for oil and a spout for the
wick. Each is set on a high, gadrooned
socle upon a canted square base. On one
lamp is a seated female figure holding a
book, on the other a woman holding a

jug. Aptly, these represent the Vestal
Virgins of ancient Rome who tended the
sacred fire in the temple of the goddess
Vesta. The layered garments are their
distinctive dress. Similar lamps were
made in the Wedgwood & Bentley
period.

64 *Plaque* c. 1860

stoneware (green jasper dip)
15.5 x 46.0 cm
Impressed mark: WEDGWOOD
Presented through The Art Foundation of
Victoria by Mr Keith M. Deutsher, Founder
Benefactor 1993   (D19-1993)

The rectangular plaque in mid-green
jasper dip is decorated in white relief

with groups of children engaged in the
pursuit of the Arts and Sciences: one
with a viol or cello, two dancers, three
with a globe, one holding a sculpted
head, two engaged in painting, and two
further musicians. The mid-19th century
production traded very much on the
reputation of Wedgwood's traditional
wares, the basalt and the jasper, with
subjects from 18th-century models.

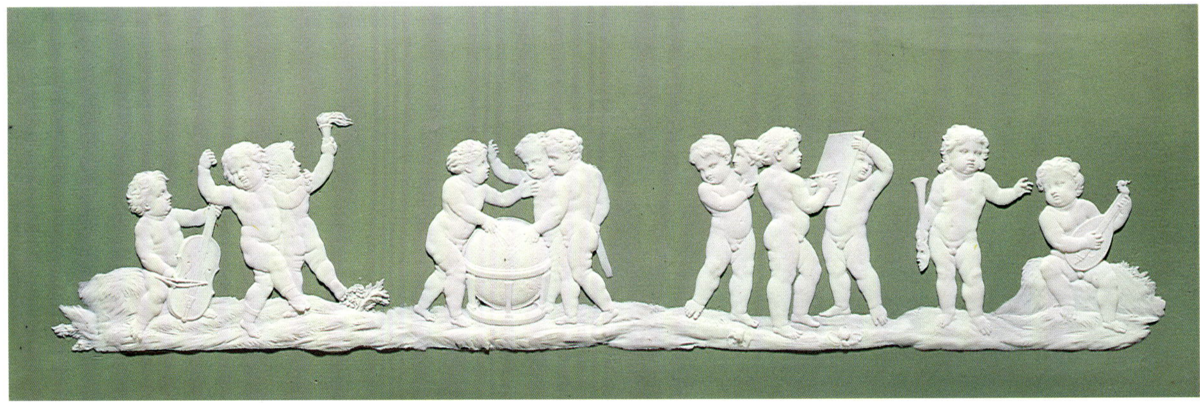

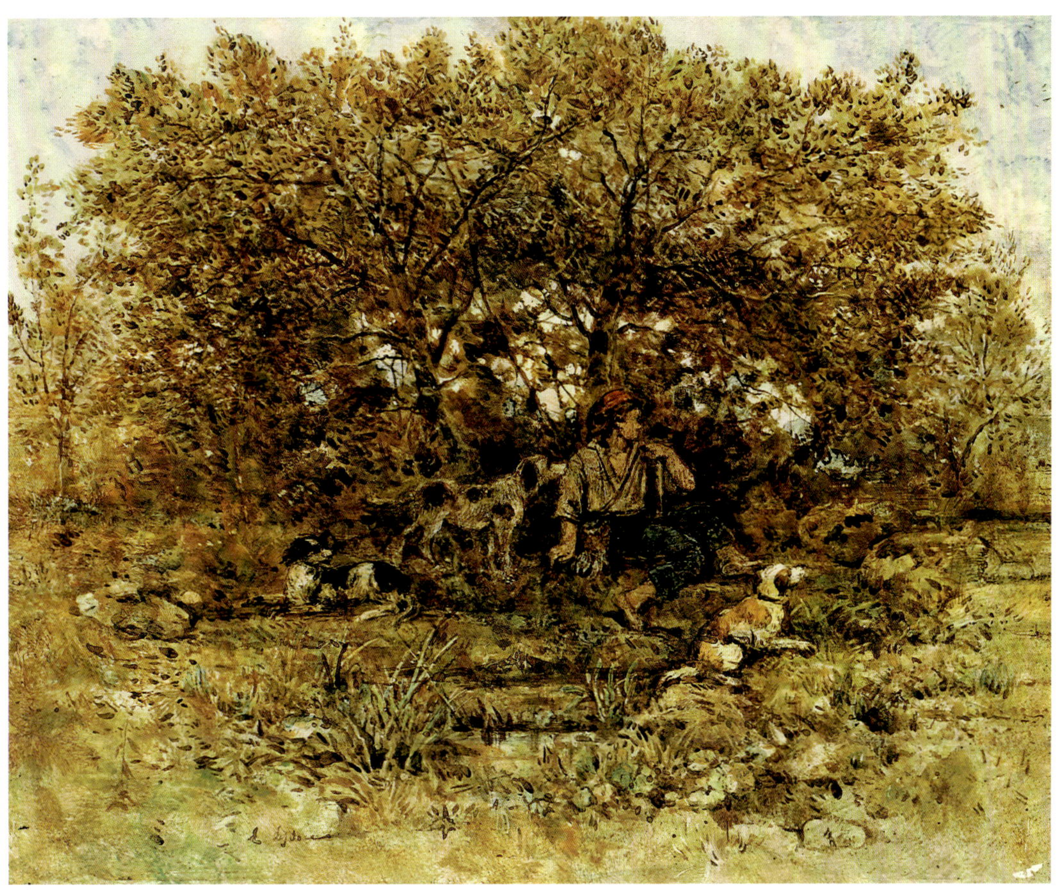

65 Plaque — *Rustic scene*
c. 1865

Painted by Emile Lessore (1805–76)
earthenware (creamware)
34.2 x 40.9 cm
signed l.l.: E. Lessore
No factory mark
Presented through The Art Foundation of
Victoria by Mrs Norma Deutsher, Governor
1994   (D39-1994)

The plaque is painted with a rustic scene
showing a shepherd and his dogs in a
wooded landscape.

Emile Lessore (1805–76) was one of
Wedgwood's most original artists. He
studied painting in France and exhibited
at the Paris Salon for 38 years. In the late
1840s he worked as a ceramic decorator
and joined the Sèvres porcelain factory in
1852. He went to England in 1858,
working firstly for Minton, where he felt
too restricted by the supervised studio
practice, and then for Wedgwood where
Francis Wedgwood allowed him the
necessary independence. He continued
to work for Wedgwood on a freelance
basis between 1863 and 1875 and after

his return to France in 1868, when he
settled at Marlotte near Fontainebleau.

The painting's style owes something
to French landscape painting of the
Barbizon school, and perhaps also to the
looser brushwork of the Impressionists.
The freshness of Lessore's sketchy style
was appreciated by his contemporaries
(see pages 13–14), whether applied to
rustic subjects or to designs derived from
Boucher, Van Dyck, Reynolds and other
Old Masters. Louis Solon,[1] who had also
worked at Minton, wrote in 1905 of
Lessore's 'bold and spirited treatment'
and told how he quite consciously
worked in quantity and in an economical
way to produce 'an article of trade'.

Lessore exhibited ceramics at the
International Exhibitions of 1862, 1867
and 1873. The retailer Mortlock bought
Wedgwood's remaining Lessore stock
after the artist's death in 1876.

NOTE

1   Quoted in Butcher (1964) pp. 215–16.

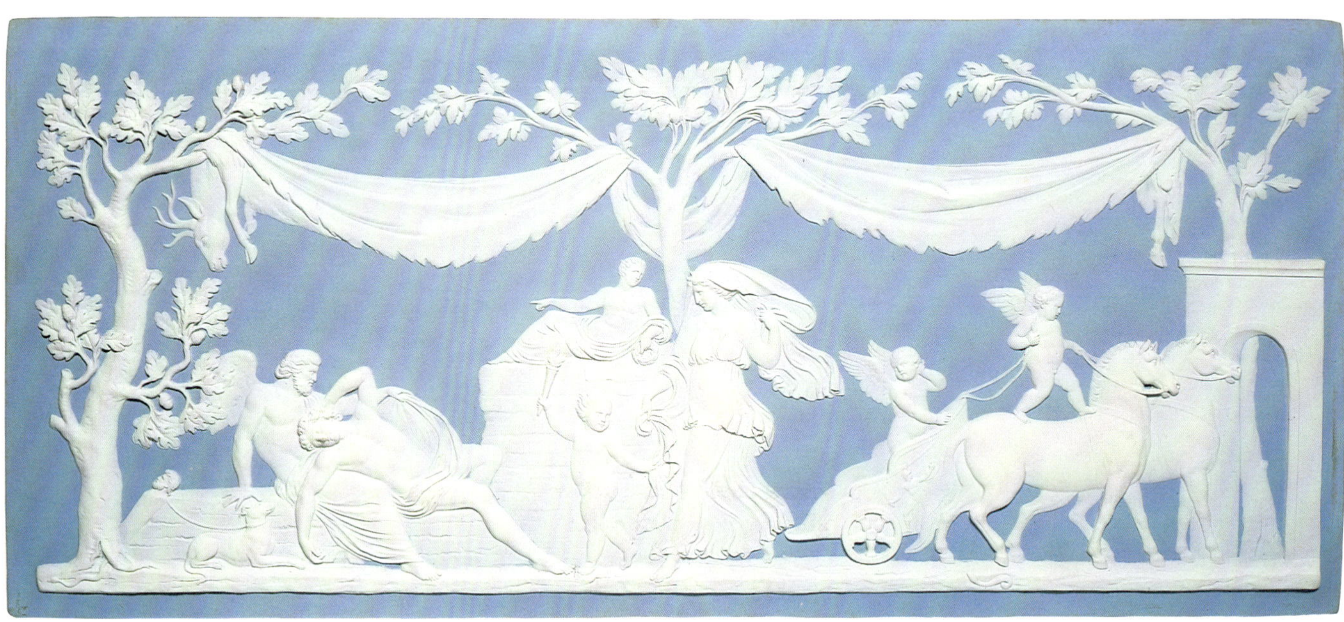

66 Plaque — Diana visiting
Endymion c. 1875

stoneware (blue jasper)
33.9 x 75.3 cm
Impressed mark: WEDGWOOD; and circle
Felton Bequest 1915 (1777-3)

This unusually large plaque shows the
moon goddess Diana, attended by
Cupids, stepping from her chariot to visit
the shepherd boy Endymion on Latmos.
The male figure in the background
probably personifies the mountain.
Endymion is shown sleeping in the lap of
Time, since the immortal goddess who
loved him did not have the power to
confer immortality upon him. The design
is framed with trees festooned with the
skins of stags, attributes proper to Diana
the Huntress. In the *Catalogue* of 1787, it
was described as 'From the celebrated
bas-relief in the Capitol at Rome' (the
sarcophagus of Gerontia).

This example is in solid light-blue
jasper with a slightly brighter blue
surface, a little more lilac in tone than
18th-century jasper. It was purchased by
the Gallery from Wedgwood's agent
Thomas Webb & Sons, Melbourne, in
1915 for £84. A rare parallel example in
the Wedgwood Museum (green jasper
dip) has been dated about 1875. A
smaller blue example was published as
probably dated 1789.[1]

NOTE

1   Rathbone (1898) pl. XXXIII.

67 Ewer — War
and Peace c. 1878

Model by Charles Toft (1832–1909)
stoneware (black jasper dip)
63.8 x 30.6 x 25.0 cm
Impressed mark: WEDGWOOD
K. and N. Deutsher collection

This monumental ewer was designed for
the Paris Exhibition of 1878 and
decorated (in relief on black jasper dip)
with allegories of War and Peace.
Though depicted in classical style, the
subjects would have been understood in
the context of the recent Franco-
German war. There was a notable French
presence in English potteries in the 19th
century, with L.M. Solon at Minton's,
Lessore at Wedgwood, and Carrier de
Belleuse and Hughes Protât at both.[1]

The tall form with its handle in the
shape of a winged female figure, its
curving rim and grotesque masks, shows
the artist's interest in Renaissance
metalwork, and particularly echoes
Parisian Renaissance Revival bronzes of
the mid-19th century.

Charles Toft (1832–1909) joined
Wedgwood in November 1876 and
became the principal figure modeller. He
had previously worked at Minton's where
he designed their 'Henri Deux' inlaid
ware in the style of the 16th-century
French pottery of St Porchaire. For
Wedgwood he produced inlaid wares and
a modified version of *pâte-sur-pâte* (relief

modelling with liquid clay, developed by
Solon for Minton) as well as original
designs in Wedgwood's own jasper relief
technique.

The ewer is rare. Records show that
four *War and Peace* vases were fired in
November 1880.[2] Two vases of this
shape, but different in technique and
decoration,[3] were in Wedgwood's display
at the Melbourne International Exhibition
in 1880 (see illustration p. 13).

NOTES

1   Protât followed Carrier de Belleuse at
    Minton (c. 1855) and was Toft's
    predecessor at Wedgwood.
2   Reilly (1989) vol. II, p. 527-8, fig. 909.
3   They appear to have been decorated in a
    black and cream scheme on creamware.
    Compare Reilly (1989) vol. II, pl. C13.

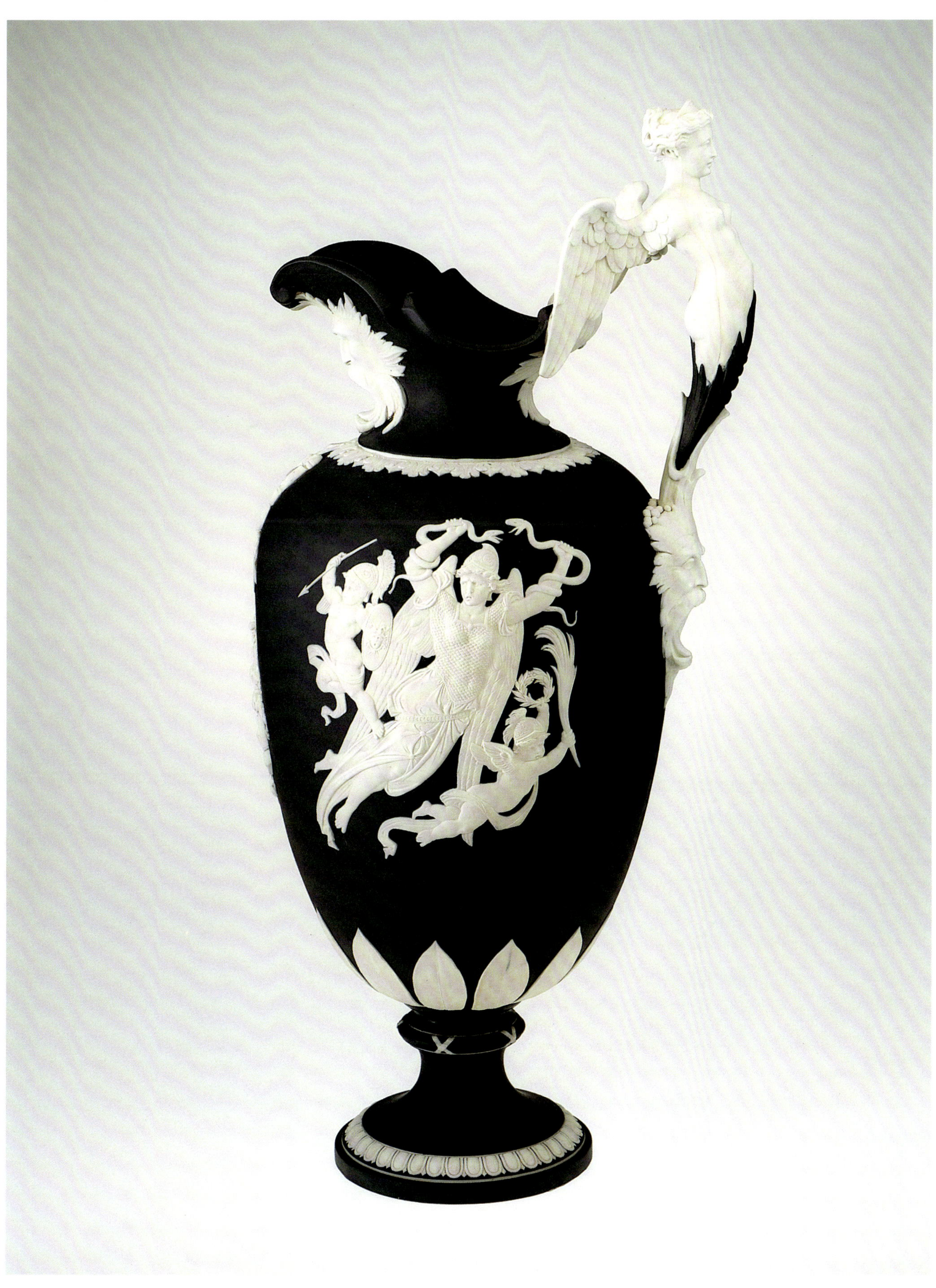

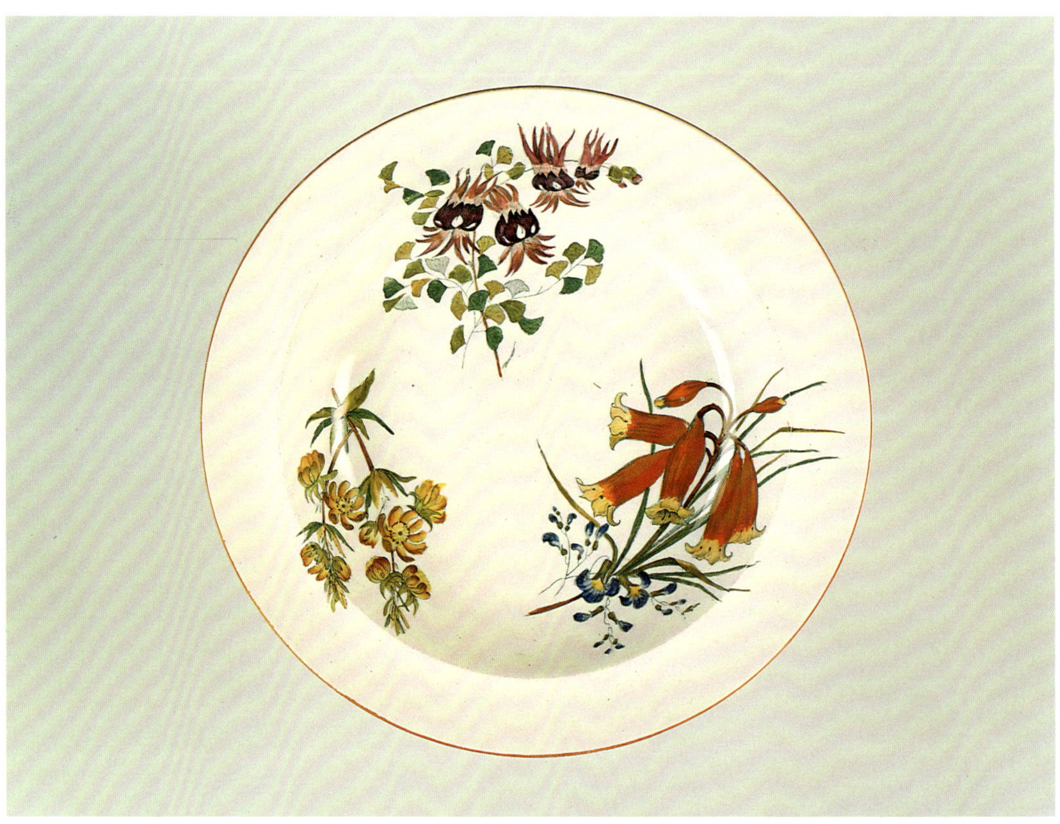

68 *Plate — 'Australian flora' pattern* c. 1880

earthenware (creamware)
24.6 x 24.6 x 3.6 cm
Impressed mark: WEDGWOOD
Mark printed in green: Australian Flora
Painted in red: A1923/a.
Presented by the Melbourne Branch of the
Australian Decorative and Fine Arts Society to
mark the Australian Bicentennial 1988
(D89-1987)

The soup plate is transfer-printed in
green and hand-coloured with three
sprays of Australian wildflowers:
Christmas bells *(Blandfordia nobilis);*
Sturt's desert pea *(Clianthus formosa)*
entwined with maidenhair fern
(Adianthum aithiopicum); and tall lobelia
(Lobelia gibbosa) combined with what is
possibly wiry bauera *(Bauera rubiodes)*.[1]
The plants seem to be copied from a
black and white botanical illustration,
since the colouring is inconsistent with
nature. The 'Australian Flora' dinnerware
was first made in 1871. There are 21
different pattern numbers in the series.[2]

NOTES
1   The identification of the flowers is given in
    Robb (1988).
2   Adeney & Landis (1982); Landis (1985)
    p. 122.

69 *Garden seat* 1886

earthenware (majolica)
41.9 x 33.4 x 32.5 cm
Impressed mark: WEDGWOOD / M / AGO
Painted in blue: 9[.]M / 2157; and stroke
Purchased with the assistance of the Century
Fund of the National Gallery Society of
Victoria 1984   (D17-1984)

The ceramic seat has imitation buttoned
upholstery in olive green, finished with a
simulated rope and tassels in pink.
Fluttering birds perch on prunus
branches between four partly open fans.
The seat would have been ideally placed
in a conservatory.
    The design reflects the widespread
interest in all things Japanese which
characterised the Aesthetic Movement,
following the reopening of contacts with
Japan in 1853 and especially from
European exposure to the decorative
arts of Japan at the London International
Exhibition of 1862. The 'Fan' pattern was
first registered in February 1879, and an
example of this seat was exhibited by
Wedgwood in Melbourne at the
International Exhibition in 1880.
    The seat is a good example of
Wedgwood's majolica, a type of glazed
earthenware made in the 19th century in

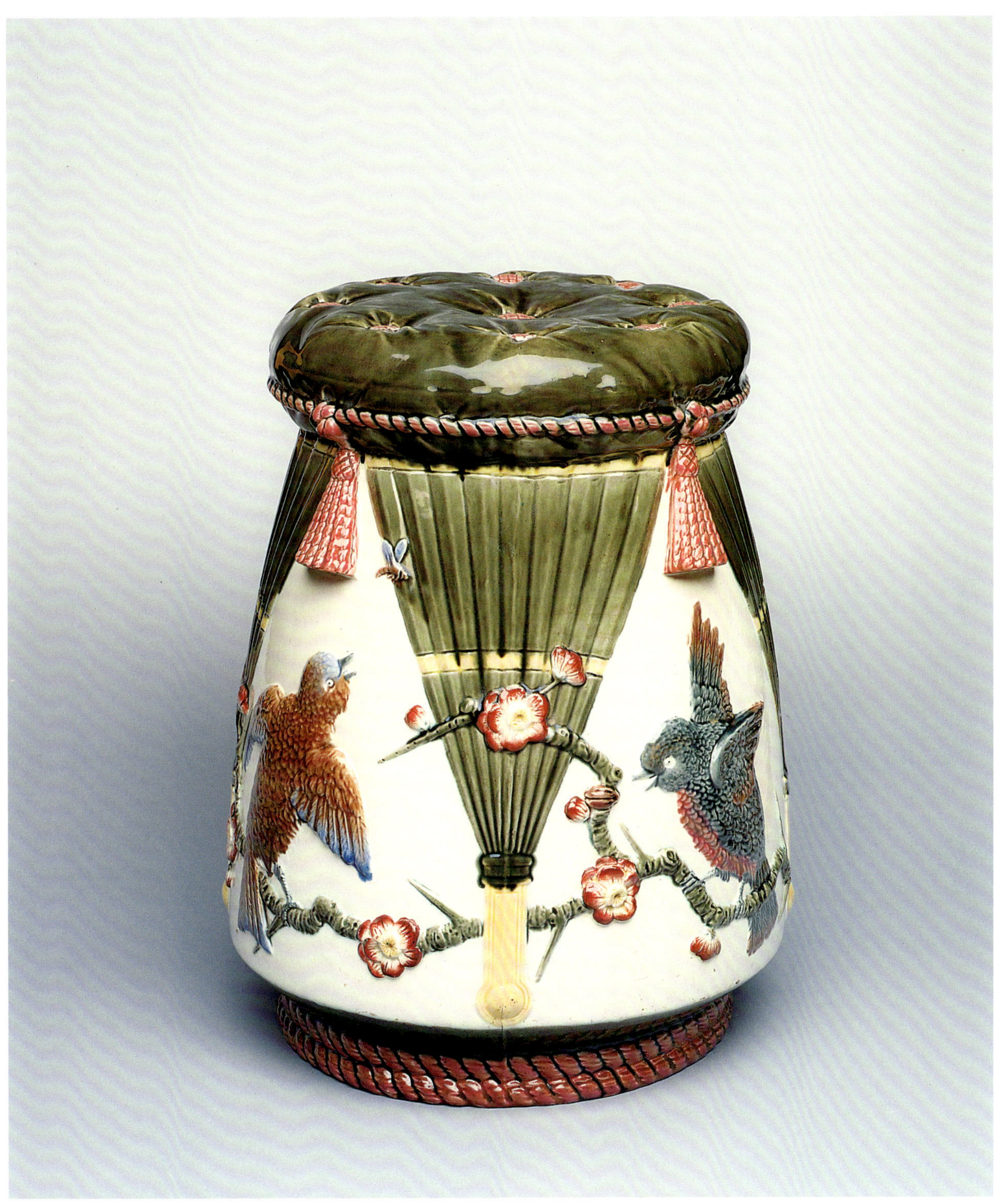

emulation of the brightly coloured 'maiolica' of the Renaissance.

The technique, which was introduced earlier at Minton's, involved painting lead-based coloured glazes onto the biscuit-fired ware, which was then fired again in the range 900º–1500ºC. It did not involve a coat of white tin-glaze as in the Renaissance. Technically and stylistically, it was often closer to the French Renaissance pottery of Bernard Palissy than to Italian 'maiolica'. Renaissance wares were being collected at the time by the new South Kensington (now Victoria and Albert) Museum.

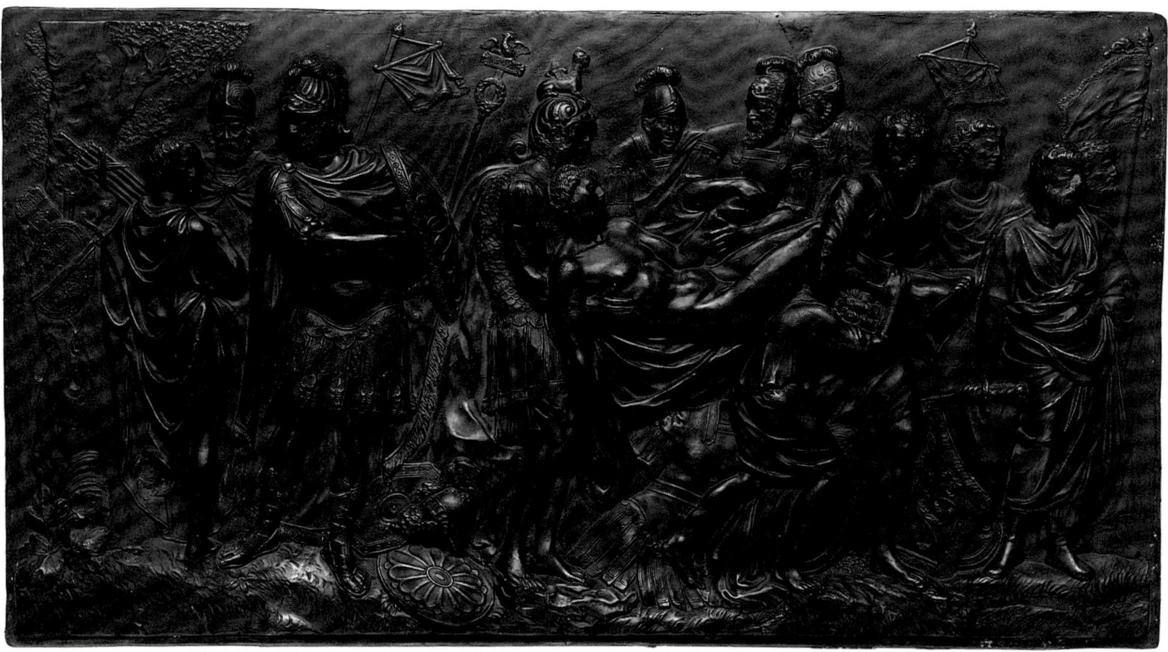

70 *Plaque — Death of a Roman Warrior* before 1887

stoneware (basalt)
Impressed mark: WEDGWOOD
Purchased 1887   (247-1)

The plaque depicts a battle scene with warriors in Roman armour, the main group showing a warrior being carried from the field, the figures in high and low relief. The design first appeared in the *Catalogue* of 1773.

This sort of large basalt panel or 'tablet' was designed in the 18th century for incorporation into architectural schemes, often as central features of Adam-style painted wall decoration. Such plaques were produced again in the 19th century and were exhibited in 1862. The present plaque is moulded in sections, with the parts in high relief added separately. The back is uneven, its hollow shape supported by pellets of clay. Although this technique suggests an 18th-century date, the quality of finish makes it more likely to be a 19th-century work.

The composition has several antique sources. The figure group with a dead warrior, also known as the *Death of Meleager,* comes from an antique sarcophagus in the Capitoline Museum, Rome. (It was formerly in the Albani collection).[1] This composition is of a type which inspired Raphael in his famous *Deposition* in the Borghese Gallery, Rome. Already in the 15th century the theorist Leon Battista Alberti had singled out for praise the expressive qualities of the composition.

The plaque was purchased by the Gallery in 1887, together with its companion piece *A Roman procession,* from Mr R.J. Carter, Sydney, for £52/10/- the pair.

NOTE

1   See Macht (1957) pp. 81–4 for further sources.

71 *Borghese vase and pedestal* c. 1888

stoneware (black jasper dip)
vase   51.7 x 29.5 x 29.5 cm
Impressed mark: WEDGWOOD
pedestal   28.9 x 28.3 x 28.3 cm
Impressed mark : WEDGWOOD
Purchased 1889   (248-1)

The campana-shaped vase in black jasper dip derives from a famous antique marble vase formerly in the collection of the Borghese family in Rome and now in the Louvre Museum. In 1788 its relief decoration of Bacchic revellers was modelled for Wedgwood by John Devaere (active about 1785–1810) who worked in Rome under the direction of John Flaxman. (The original wax model is in Nottingham Castle Museum). The pedestal shape is similar to that of the *Homer vase* (see cat. no. 44).

The original Borghese vase was illustrated by Montfaucon and others and there were full-scale replicas in many important English collections, such as at Houghton Hall and Osterley Park. It was copied in bronze and in artificial stone in the 18th century, and made into silver gilt wine coolers by Paul Storr for the Prince Regent in 1808. The two handles seen on the Wedgwood version were often added to make the vase a pair with another famous antique, the Medici vase.

The Wedgwood vase was purchased for £35 by the Gallery from Messrs T. Webb & Sons at the time of the Centennial International Exhibition in Melbourne in 1888, one hundred years after Wedgwood received Devaere's model. It would have been well suited to the eclectic decorative scheme of an Italianate villa of Melbourne in the 1880s.

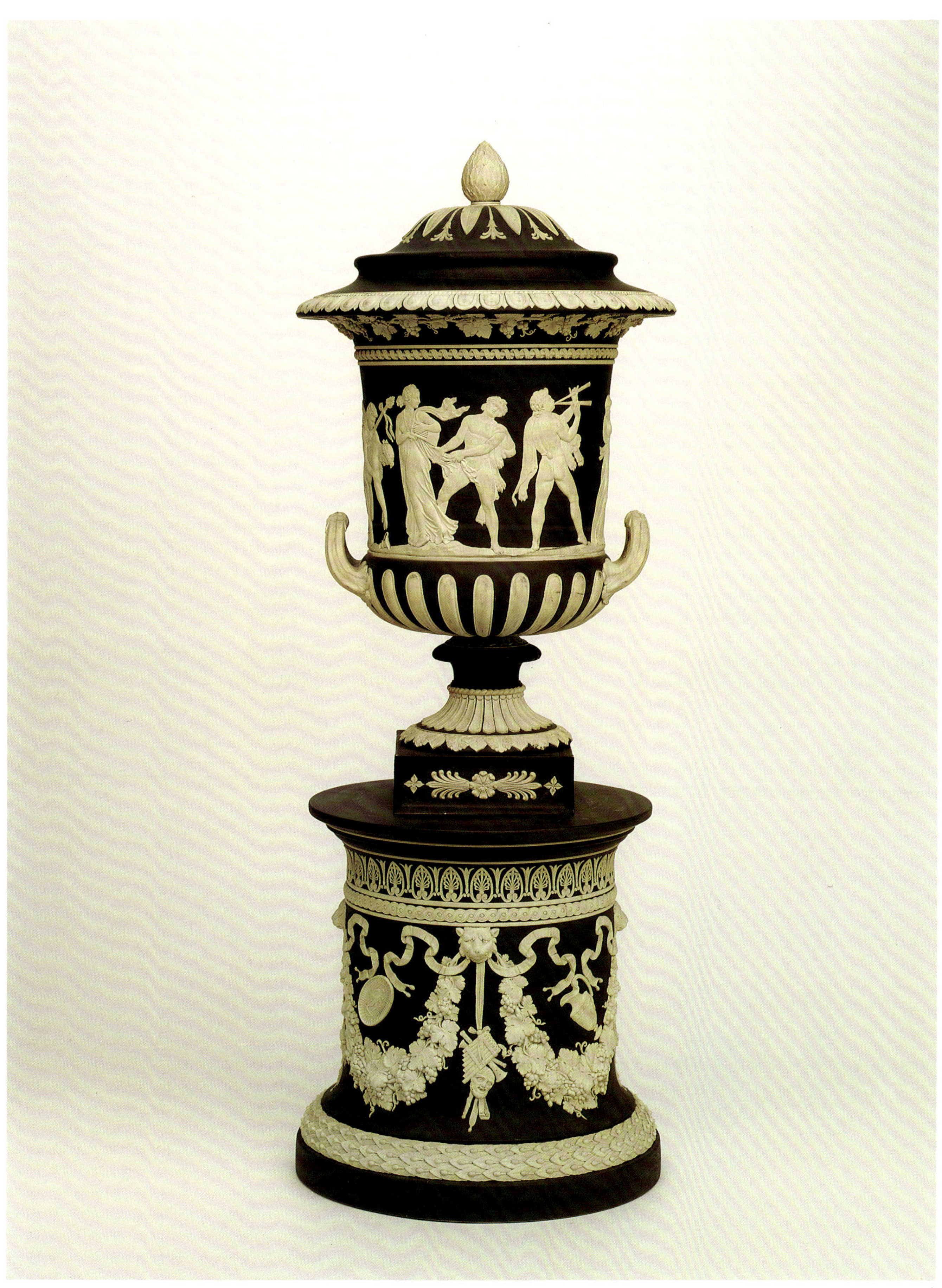

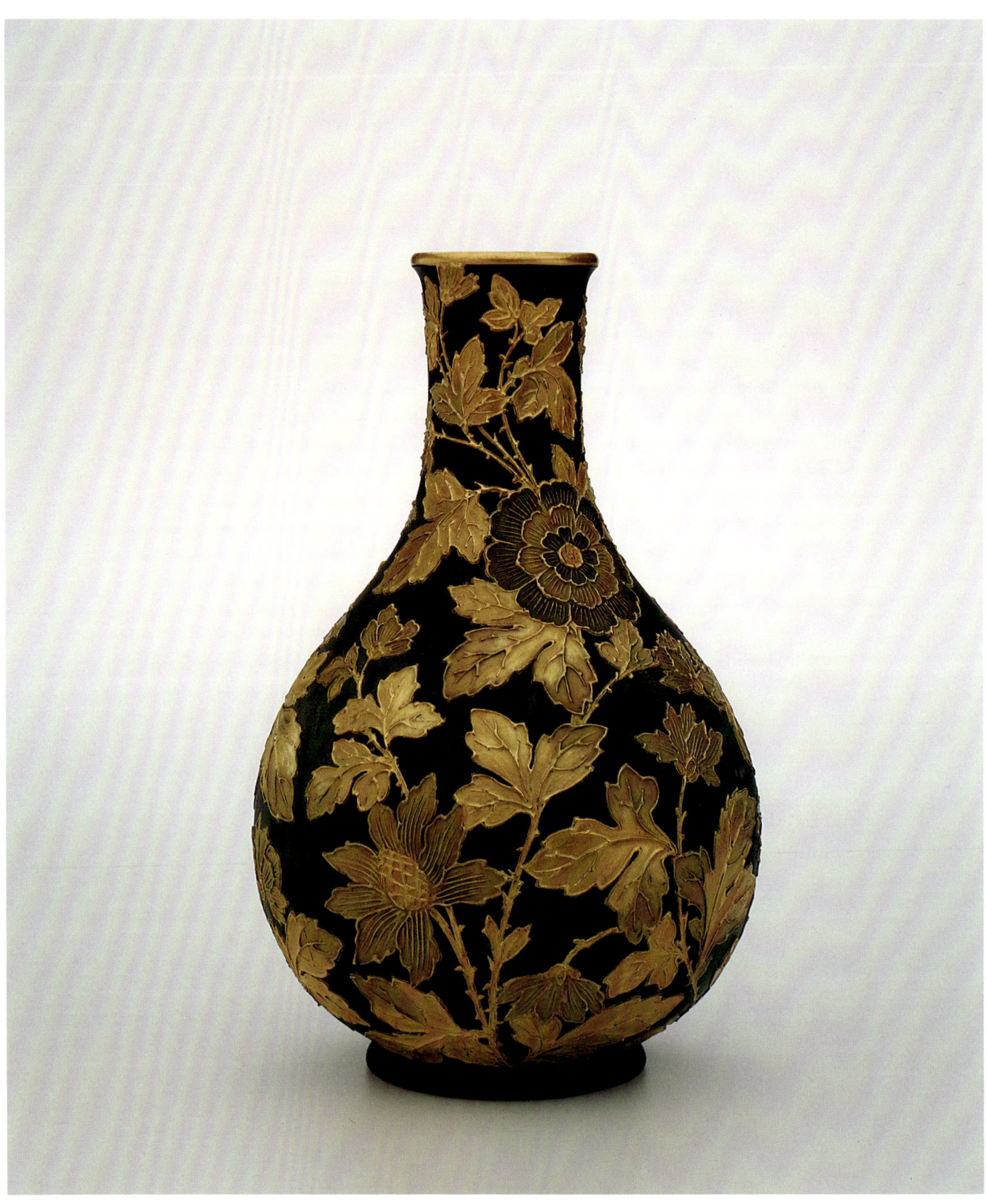

72 *Vase* c. 1888

stoneware (aurobasalt)
33.5 x 20.9 x 20.9 cm
Impressed mark: WEDGWOOD; and split
circle
Incised: S.628
Purchased 1889   (249-1)

The design of leaves and flowers is
executed in gilded raised paste: the
outlines in relief were applied using slip
and the gilding was executed in different
shades of gold against the black ground.
There are also details in pale red glaze.

This type of ware, called 'aurobasalt',
was introduced in about 1885, and was
influenced by Japanese partly gilt bronze
vases. (For *japonisme* see also cat. no.
69.) The simple fluid shape was inspired
by oriental ceramics, while the rich
decoration has an unusual 'all-over'
effect, like a textile design.

This vase was purchased by the
Gallery from Messrs T. Webb & Sons at
the time of the Centennial International
Exhibition in Melbourne in 1888 for
£5/10/-.

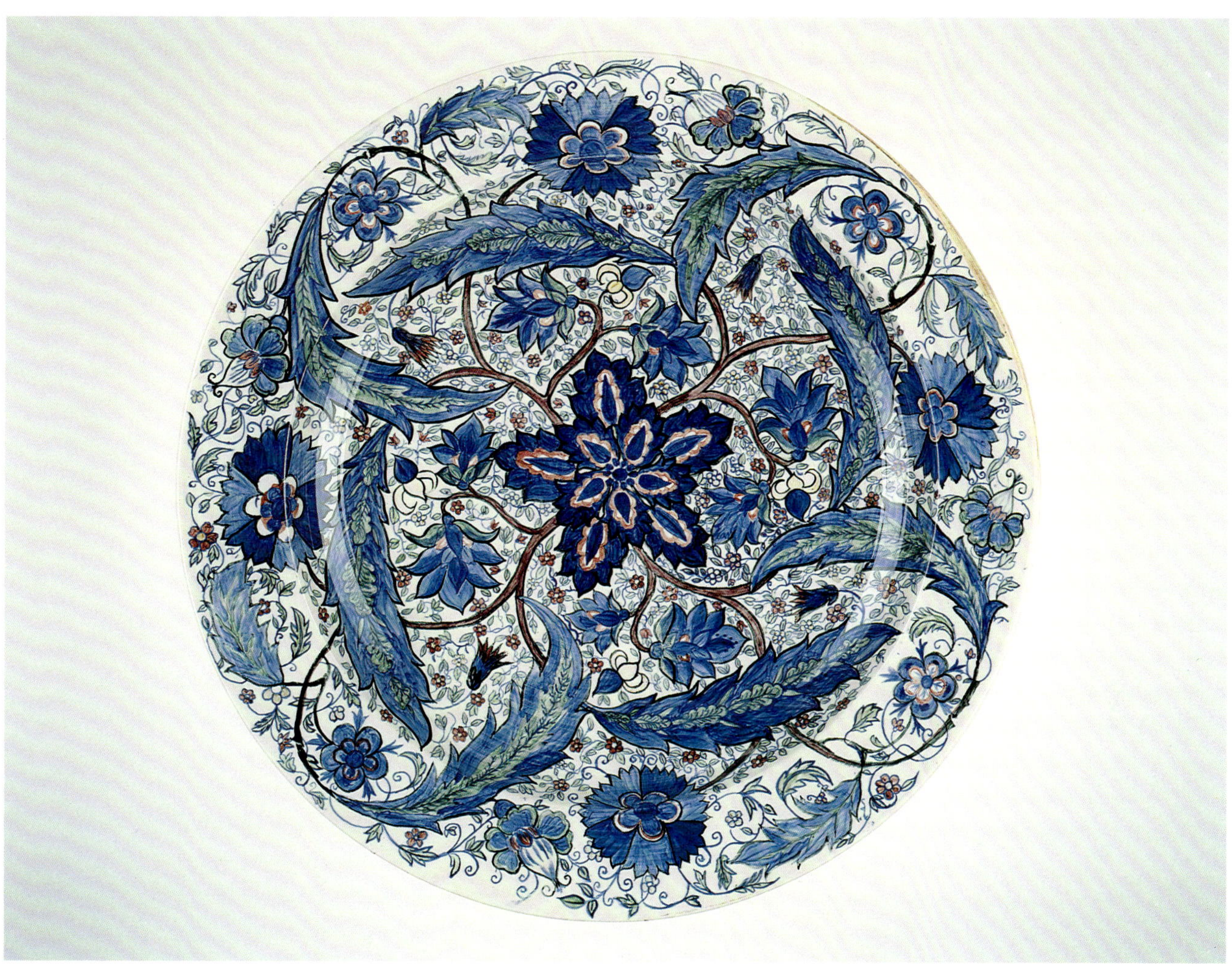

73 *Large dish* 1909

Painted in the style of Alfred and Louise
Powell
earthenware (creamware)
55.7 x 55.7 x 8.7 cm
Impressed mark: WEDGWOOD / S / 3DL
Painted mark in blue: L
K. and N. Deutsher collection

The large dish is decorated with stlylised
flowers and foliage in dark and light blue,
green and pink, arranged in an interesting
combination of four- and five-fold
symmetry.

The boldly decorative design stems
from Turkish Isnik pottery, which was at
its height in the 16th century. It was
much admired in the 19th century, when
it was known as 'Rhodian' or 'Damascus'
ware. The French potter Théodore Deck
showed studio pottery in this style at the
Paris Exhibition of 1861. In England
William de Morgan was its leading
exponent from the 1870s, when he made
tiles for the Arab Hall of Leighton House,
until the closure of his studio in 1907.
The style was popular within the context
of the Art and Crafts Movement.

Wedgwood's venture into the Arts
and Crafts style was through the
company's cooperation with Alfred and
Louise Powell. This began with Alfred
Powell (1865–1960) supplying designs to
the Etruria works in 1903,[1] and in the
1920s resulted in a revival of hand-
painting at the factory under the
direction of Millicent Taplin (1902–80),
whom Powell had trained.

In 1906 Alfred Powell married Ada
Louise Lessore (1882–1956), grand-
daughter of Emile Lessore (see cat. no.
65), and early in 1907 they established a
studio in Bloomsbury, exhibiting wares
which they and other Arts and Crafts
designers had painted and designed. At
this time Wedgwood supplied blanks
from the factory, which were painted and
fired in London. The Powells worked
closely together, but Louise, trained in
calligraphy and illumination at the Central
School of Art, is particulary associated
with the calligraphic Islamic designs.
Alfred Powell was concerned with the
shapes of the wares as well as the
decoration. In 1906 he asked for
Wedgwood's shapes to be modified,[2]
preferring a natural hand-crafted look to
the tightly controlled finish of factory
production. The present dish shows the
circular ridges ('throwing rings') created
by the potter; these would normally be
smoothed away. This free way of working
the clay is sympathetic to the hand-
painted character of the design.

NOTES

1   The *Art Journal* review of Powell's 1906
    exhibition at Grafton Galleries considered
    his emergence a counterbalance to the
    loss of William de Morgan.
2   Letters from Frank Wedgwood to Powell
    quoted in Batkin (1982) p. 142.

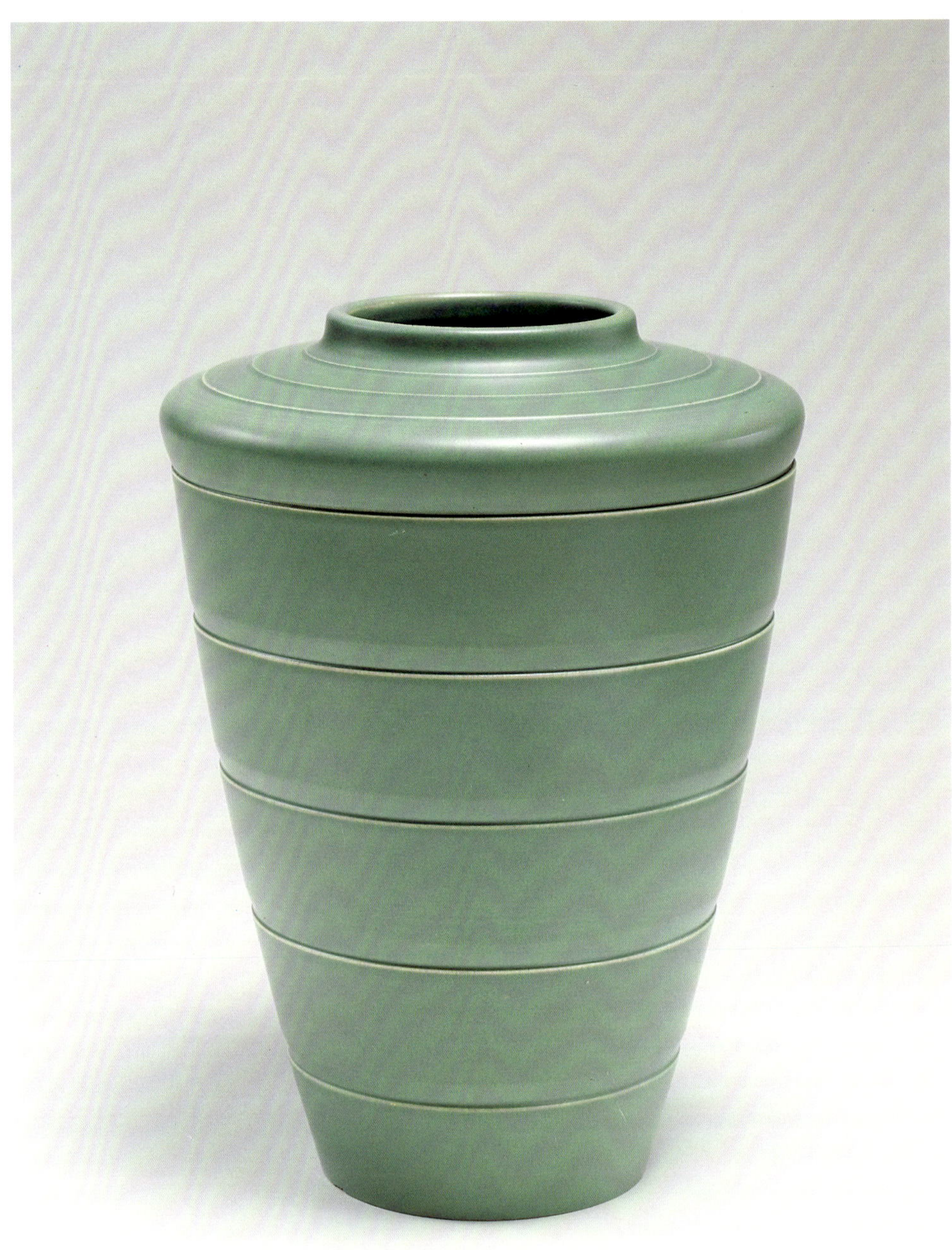

74 *Vase* c. 1935

Design by Keith Murray (1892–1981)
earthenware
28.4 x 20.4 x 20.4 cm
Impressed: WEDGWOOD [sans
serif] / E / H / MADE IN ENGLAND
Printed in black: Keith Murray [in
script], WEDGWOOD / MADE IN
ENGLAND / MATT GREEN
Gift of The Wedgwood Society of
Australia 1994

The tapered body of the vase is decorated with a series of sharply defined turned grooves which cause the matt green glaze to 'break' to a lighter colour. Keith Murray's work for Wedgwood was in the vanguard of 20th-century British ceramic design. Its geometric simplicity, complemented by the new matt glazes developed by art director Norman Wilson, constituted the most radical strain of Wedgwood's modernism of the 1930s.

Keith Murray was born in Auckland, New Zealand in 1892 and went to England in 1906–7. After serving in the Air Force (1915–18) he studied at the Architectural Association School in London. As there was little opportunity for architects in the 1920s and '30s, he turned to industrial design.

Murray began his association with Wedgwood in 1932 and by the end of 1934 had created well over a hundred new shapes. Many of these remained in production until the late 1950s. In the 1930s Murray also designed glassware (for Stevens and Williams, Stourbridge), and silver (for Mappin and Webb). He was influenced by the Scandinavian and other modern European design seen at the *Exposition Internationale des Arts Décoratifs* in Paris in 1925 (origin of the term 'Art Deco').

Murray's Wedgwood was first shown in the important exhibition *British Industrial Art in Relation to the Home*, at Dorland Hall, London, in 1933. He attracted special attention at the Royal Academy exhibition in 1935 and also showed his designs internationally. With his partner C.S. White he designed the new Wedgwood factory which opened at Barlaston in 1940, and from 1948 to 1967 he devoted himself to architecture with his firm Murray, Ward and Partners.

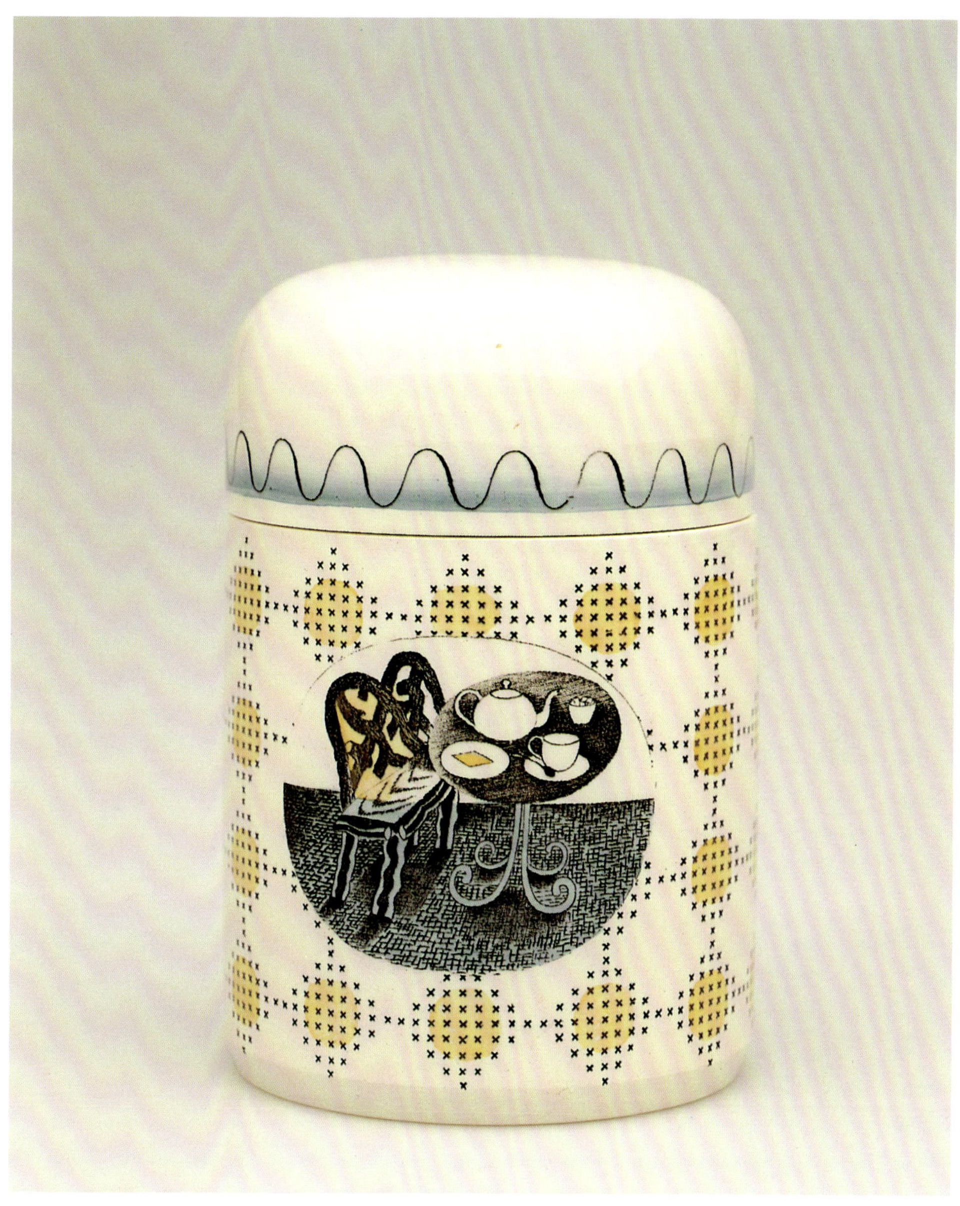

75 *Preserve jar — 'Afternoon tea' pattern* 1940s

Design by Eric Ravilious (1903–42), c. 1938
earthenware
13.4 x 8.8 x 8.8 cm
Printed mark in black: Designed / by Eric /
Ravilious
Painted in red: CL 6266 / 12
Felton Bequest 1949   (923-4)

The lidded jar is printed in black with a
diagonal checkerboard pattern and with a
vignette showing a table set for tea. The
design is finished with simple but effective
touches of blue and yellow.

Eric Ravilious studied at the
Eastbourne and Brighton Schools of Art
and in 1922 went to the Royal College
where he was taught by Paul Nash

(1889–1946), a painter who also made
important contributions to industrial
design. Ravilious himself was a painter,
particularly in watercolour, and a graphic
artist. His stylish book illustrations used
the technique of wood engraving, which
was enjoying a revival in Britain in the
1930s. Ravilious provided designs for the
1934 Harrods exhibition of ceramics by
27 leading artists who were invited to
bring their skills to the decoration of
table wares. He was connected with the
London retail shop Dunbar Hay and,
through its manager Lady Cecilia Sempill,
met Tom Wedgwood. He designed for
Wedgwood in 1937 and 1938. Ravilious
produced elegant linear work which
combined gentle humour and the sort of
simplicity found in folk art with a high

degree of visual sophistication and an
interest in Surrealism. He died while
acting as a war artist.

The Gallery has a substantial group of
his Wedgwood wares, including the well-
known *Boat race bowl* (where scenes of
modern urban life combine with
mermaids) and a lemonade jug of the
traditional 'Liverpool' shape (seen in
18th-century creamware). The latter is
painted with the 'Garden implements'
pattern which has elements similar to
those on the early Wedgwood jug (cat.
no. 8). He preserved the spirit of the
early creamwares in a distinctively
modern way.

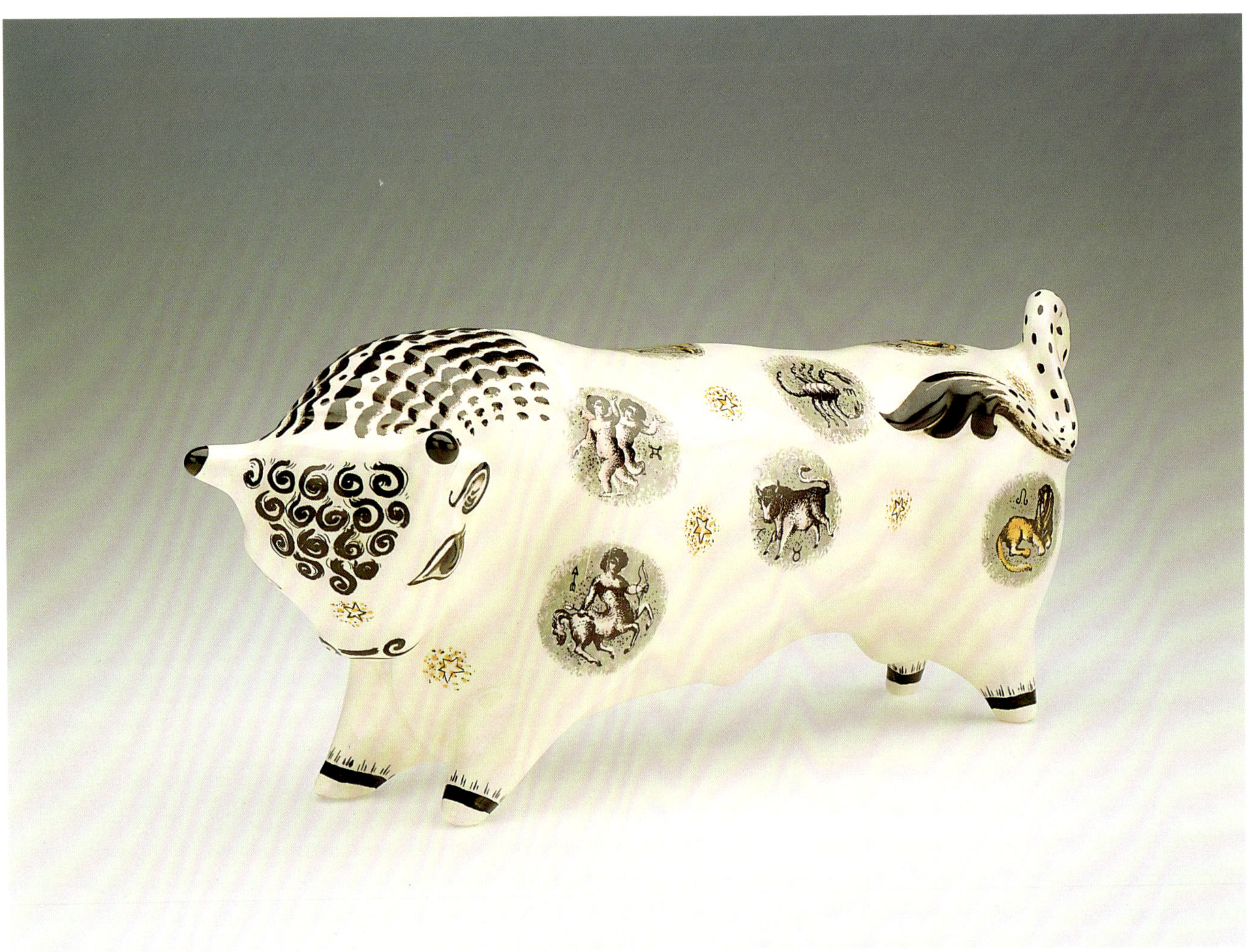

76 *Zodiac bull* 1954

Model by Arnold Machin (b. 1911), 1945
earthenware
16.0 x 40.2 x 15.4 cm
Printed in green (partly obscured):
WEDG[WOOD] / BARLA[STON]../
ENGL[AND]
Impressed mark: 12 U 54 / WEDGWOOD
Bequest of Mrs Stella Hawkes 1991
(D60-1991)

Machin's *Bull* is regarded as a classic of modern British design,[1] created expressly to make the best use of the semi-skilled labour available during the war years. Arnold Machin designed an easily cast model and drew directly on the lithographic plates to create the eyes, nostrils and other decoration which could then be printed quite simply. The body has stars and roundels showing the signs of the Zodiac printed in brown, grey, pink and yellow.

Its modernism is a forerunner of the style of the Festival of Britain in 1951 which introduced the wider British public to modern design concepts after the austerities of the 1940s.

Arnold Machin studied at the Royal College of Art, London. He worked with ceramics at Minton's in 1930, then at Royal Crown Derby and at Worcester, and was later concerned with the design of postage stamps and coinage (in the 1950s and '60s respectively). In 1940 Josiah Wedgwood, current namesake of the founder of the company, was looking for 'a Ravilious in clay', and accepted Machin on the recommendation of his contacts at the Royal College of Art.

He occupied a studio, separate from the factory, where he made large-scale sculpture and works in terracotta as well as models for production. On 22 April 1941 Wedgwood observed that '… we have found that we get the best results by giving him an entirely free hand'. The artist–designer obviously understood the strictures of the pottery business.

Machin's ceramic figures were fresh and even humorous, reinterpreting the traditional Staffordshire figure. He also modelled jasper reliefs.

Note

1   Hogben (1983) p. 179.

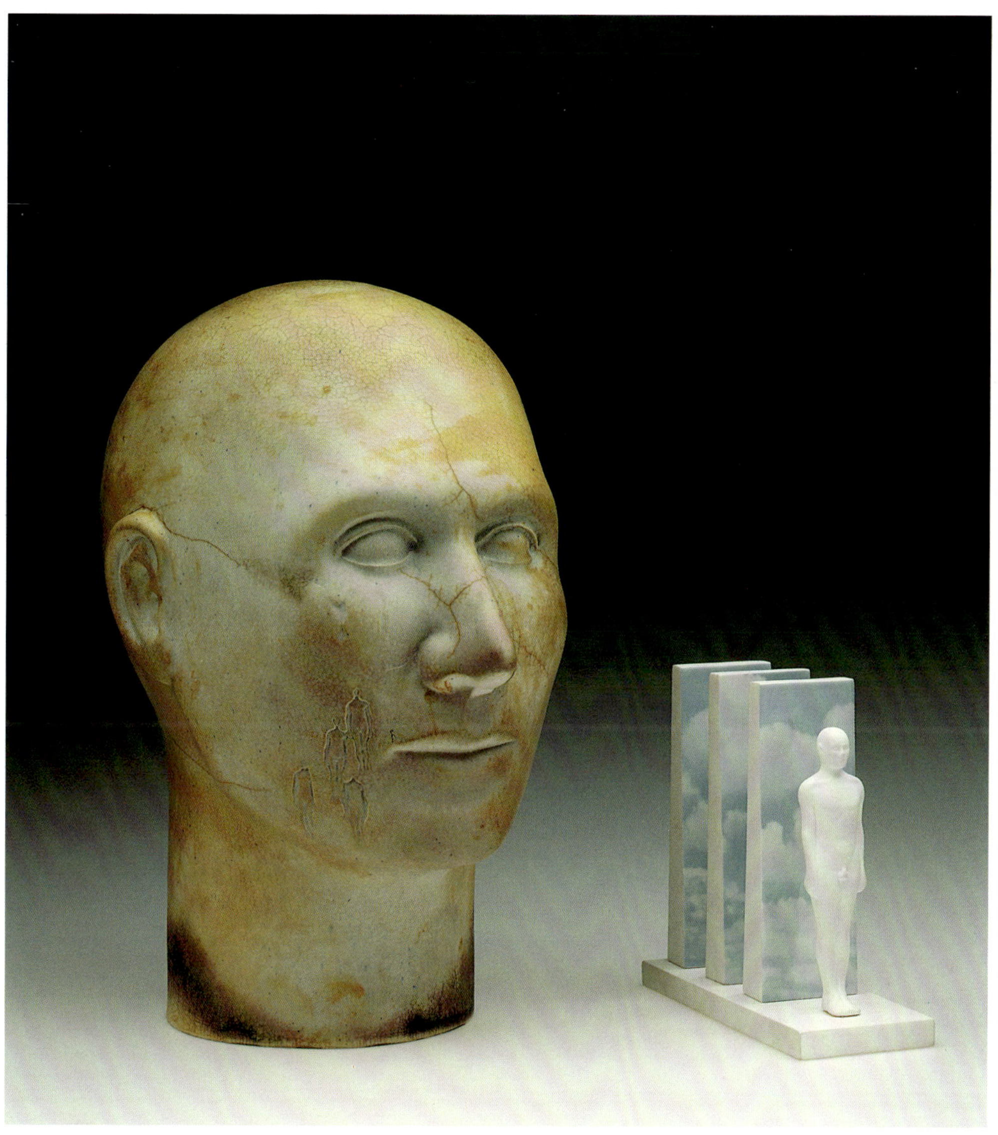

77 *Male head* c. 1976

Model by Glenys Barton (b. 1944), 1976
semi-porcelain
37.8 x 23.4 x 29.4 cm
Unmarked
Purchased with the assistance of the Crafts
Board of the Australia Council 1981
(D160-1981)

The over life-size head of a man is
treated with emphatic symmetry, and tiny
figures of men and women are impressed
on its right cheek and on the back of the
skull. The mottled glaze, in tones of pale
grey, ochre and purplish pink, is
deliberately crazed through *raku* firing
and the cracks seem to have been
enhanced with colour. The form has been
slipcast (formed by pouring liquid clay
into a mould, an old Staffordshire
method now widespread in manufacture).

Wedgwood has from time to time
invited studio ceramists to make
experimental designs utilising the
factory's resources. Glenys Barton was
born in Stoke-on-Trent, and is one of an
important group of women ceramic
artists who came to notice in the 1970s
after studying with Hans Coper at the
Royal College of Art, London. They
included Alison Britton, Elizabeth Fritsch
and Jacqui Poncelet (with whom Barton
shared a studio from 1971 to 1975).
Barton was artist-in-residence at
Wedgwood in Staffordshire in 1976.
Since 1977 she has been teaching at the
Camberwell School of Art, London, and
has worked in her Essex studio since
1984.[1] She participated in the *The Portrait
Now* exhibition at the National Portrait
Gallery, London, 1993–94.

Barton has made a highly personal
language of images and allied
it with the techniques of serial
production. *Male head* was
bought following the British
Council exhibition, *Image and
Idea,* which was shown at the
Gallery in 1980.[2]

NOTES

1 Watson (1990) pp. 32, 150,
151.
2 Houston (1979). The exhibition
was shown at the National
Gallery of Victoria, 1–31
August 1980.

78 *Time at Yagul*
c. 1976

Model by Glenys Barton
(b. 1944), 1976
bone china
17.5 x 19.7 x 7.3 cm
Printed mark in blue:
WEDGWOOD / Made in
England/ TIME AT YAGUL /
Glenys Barton
Printed in black: 2
Presented by Sir Arthur Bryan,
Chairman of Josiah Wedgwood &
Sons Ltd on the occasion of the
250th anniversary of the birth of
Josiah Wedgwood 1980
(D65-1980)

The sculptural work
comprises a figure of a man
standing on a rectangular
base, behind him three
tapered slabs of sky, each silk-
screen printed with clouds in
blue. There is an eerie quality
in Barton's work, well described by John
Houston: 'The perfect execution of each
element leaves no room for doubt, or
hope'.[1] It seems to bring together
elements of Neoclassicism (the cool
abstraction and feeling for silhouette) and
the anxious imagery of Surrealism. The
abstract quality of the forms is well
matched to the silky matt surface of the
china. Like *Male head*, *Time at Yagul* was
intended for serial production. However
Barton's work for Wedgwood was only
produced in limited editions of four.

NOTE

1   Houston (1979) p. 17.

SELECT BIBLIOGRAPHY

Adeney, J. (1989) 'Incised and impressed decoration on Wedgwood', *Proceedings of the Thirty-fourth Annual Wedgwood International Seminar*, pp. 103–24.

Adeney, J.A. & Landis, A.O. (1982) 'Wedgwood wares related to Australia', *Proceedings of the Twenty-seventh Annual Wedgwood International Seminar*, pp. 83–97.

Allen, H. (1981) '"Egyptian" Wedgwood', *Proceedings of the Twenty-sixth Annual Wedgwood International Seminar*, pp. 42–71.

Barker, D. (1990) *William Greatbatch: a Staffordshire Potter*, Jonathan Horne, London.

Batkin, M. (1982) *Wedgwood Ceramics 1846–1959*, Richard Dennis, London.

Bindman, D. (ed.), (1979) *John Flaxman, R.A.*, (exh. cat.), Royal Academy of Arts, London.

Binyon, H. (1983) *Eric Ravilious: memoir of an artist*, Lutterworth Press, Guildford.

Butcher, H. (1964) 'Emile Lessore', *Proceedings of the Wedgwood International Seminar*, pp. 215–16.

Buten, D. (1980) *18th-century Wedgwood: a guide for collectors and connoisseurs*, Pitman, London.

Buten, D. & Pehelach, P. (1979) *Emile Lessore 1805–1876: his life and work*, Monographs in Wedgwood Studies, no. 3, Buten Museum of Wedgwood, Merion, Pa.

Buten, H.M. (ed.), (1967) *Wedgwood trio by Meteyard*, Buten Museum of Wedgwood, Merion, Pa. (reprint of Eliza Meteyard, *Wedgwood and his works*, 1873; *Memorials of Wedgwood*, 1874; *Choice examples of Wedgwood art*, 1879).

Buten, H.M. (1969) *Wedgwood rarities*, Buten Museum of Wedgwood, Merion, Pa.

Dawson, A. (1984) *Masterpieces of Wedgwood in the British Museum*, British Museum, London.

Deutsher, K. (1984) 'The Imperial Russian dinner and dessert service of 1774', *Wedgwood News*, vol. 12, no. 3, Wedgwood Society of Australia, Melbourne.

Drakard, D. (1986) 'Early printing at Etruria', *Proceedings of the Wedgwood Society*, no. 12, pp. 193–205.

Dukelskaya, L. (intro.), (1979) *The Hermitage: English art, sixteenth to nineteenth century*, Aurora Publishing, Leningrad.

Farrer, Lady Katherine (ed.), (1903–06) *Letters of Josiah Wedgwood*, 2 vols, privately printed 1903, and *Correspondence of Josiah Wedgwood, 1906* (reprinted with an introduction by B. Tattersall, E.J. Morten Ltd, Manchester, together with The Trustees of the Wedgwood Museum, Barlaston, Stoke-on-Trent [intro. dated 1973], 3 vols).

Fontaines, J.K. (1984) *The Wedgwood illustrated catalogue of ornamental shapes 1878*, Wedgwood Society, London.

Fontaines, U. des (1975) *Wedgwood Fairyland*

Lustre: the work of Daisy Makeig-Jones, Sotheby Parke Bernet, London.

Finer, A. & Savage, G. (1965) *The Selected Letters of Josiah Wedgwood*, Cory, Adams & Mackay Ltd, London.

Gater, S. (1982) 'Alfred and Louise Powell — an introduction', *Proceedings of the Wedgwood Society*, no. 11, pp. 153–62.

Gater, S. (1993) 'Arnold Machin O.B.E., A.R.C.A.', *Proceedings of the Wedgwood Society*, no. 14, pp. 5–13.

Grant, M.H. (1910) *The Makers of black basaltes* (reprinted The Holland Press, London, 1967).

d'Hancarville, P. [Pierre Hugues, called d'Hancarville] (1766–67) *Collection of Etruscan, Greek, and Roman Antiquities from the Cabinet of the Honble Wm Hamilton His Britannick Maiesty's Envoy Extraordinary at the Court of Naples*, Naples, 4 vols.

Haydon, P. (1986) 'British seats on Imperial Russian tables', *Proceedings of the Wedgwood Society*, no. 12, pp. 206–14.

Holdway, P. (1990) ' "Print it the glue way" … From Sadler to Spode', *Proceedings of the Thirty-fifth Annual Wedgwood International Seminar*, pp. 193–200.

Hogarth, William (1753) *The Analysis of Beauty* (new edition Joseph Burke (ed.), Clarendon Press, Oxford, 1955).

Hogben, C. (intro.), (1983) *British Art and Design 1900–1960*, Victoria and Albert Museum, London.

Honey, W.B. (1948) *Wedgwood ware*, Faber & Faber, London.

Honour, H. (1968) *Neoclassicism*, Penguin, Harmondsworth.

Houston, J. (1979) *Image and Idea: a view of contemporary ceramics in Britain*, The British Council, London (cat. of exhibition held at the National Gallery of Victoria, August 1980).

Irwin, D. (1979) *John Flaxman 1755–1826*, Studio Vista/Christie's, London.

Josiah Wedgwood, the Arts and Sciences united (exh. cat.), (1978) The Science Museum, London.

Johnson, H.A. (1990) 'Books belonging to Wedgwood & Bentley the 10th of Augt 1770', *Ars Ceramica*, no. 7, pp. 13–23.

Johnson, H.A. (1991) 'Further research', *Ars Ceramica*, no. 8, p. 34.

Kelly, A. (1965) *Decorative Wedgwood in architecture and furniture*, Country Life Ltd, London.

Kelly, A. (1980) 'Wedgwood's Catherine services', *Burlington Magazine,* vol. 122, no. 929, pp. 554–61 & figs 14–32.

Landis, A. (1985) 'Wedgwood and Australia', *Australian Business Collector's Annual*, p. 122.

Macht, C. (1957) *Classical Wedgwood Designs*, M. Barrows & Co., New York.

The Man at Hyde Park Corner: sculpture by John Cheere 1709–1787 (exh. cat.), (1974) Temple Newsam, Leeds.

Mankowitz, W. (1952) *The Portland Vase and the Wedgwood copies*, André Deutsch, London.

Meteyard E. (1865) *The Life of Josiah Wedgwood*, Hurst & Blackett, London, 2 vols.

Montfaucon, Bernard de (1722) *L'Antiquité expliquée et representée en figures*, Paris, 5 vols; (1724) *Supplement*, Paris, 5 vols.

Pulver, M. (1986) 'Arnold Machin and the Wedgwood connection', *Ars Ceramica*, no. 3, 1986, pp. 16–19.

Raeburn, M. (1990) 'Land of the free: the views on the Green Frog service', *Proceedings of the Wedgwood International Seminar*, pp. 21–39.

Rakow, L.S. & Rakow, J.K. (1981) 'Marks — Good, bad and indifferent', *Proceedings of the Twenty-sixth Annual Wedgwood International Seminar*, pp. 129–59.

Rakow, L.S. & Rakow, J.K. (1986) 'Wedgwood pâte-sur-pâte', *Proceedings of the Wedgwood Society*, no. 12, pp. 228–41.

Ramage, N.H. (1991) 'Publication dates of Sir William Hamilton's four volumes', *Ars Ceramica*, no. 8, pp. 35–6.

Rathbone, F. (1898) *Old Wedgwood*, Bernard Quaritch, London (reprinted H. Buten (ed.), Buten Museum of Wedgwood, Merion, Pa., 1968).

Reilly, R. (1989) *Wedgwood*, Macmillan, London, 2 vols.

Reilly, R. & Savage, G. (1973) *Wedgwood, the portrait medallions*, Barrie & Jenkins, London.

Reilly, R. & Savage, G. (1980), *The Dictionary of Wedgwood*, Antique Collectors' Club Ltd, Woodbridge, UK.

Robb, G. (1988) 'Wedgwood and wildflowers', *Gallery*, National Gallery Society of Victoria, September, p. 28.

Roberts, G. Blake et al. (1984) *Wedgwood in London, 225th Anniversary Exhibition 1759–1984* (exh. cat.), Josiah Wedgwood & Sons Ltd, London.

Roberts, G. Blake (1986a) 'The Wedgwood School in Rome', *Proceedings of the Wedgwood Society*, no. 12, pp. 215–27.

Roberts, G. Blake (1986b) 'We fear no rivals', *Proceedings of the Wedgwood Society*, no. 12, pp. 242–53.

Roberts, G. Blake (1990) 'Patterns of trade in the 18th century', *English Ceramic Circle*, vol. 14, part 1, pp. 93–105.

Roberts, G. Blake (1993) 'Ceramics unsung hero — Thomas Bentley', *English Ceramic Circle*, vol. 15, pt 1, pp. 24–36.

Roberts, G. Blake, Halfpenny, P. & Miller, L. (1994) 'Wedgwood & Bentley: the art of deception', *Ars Ceramica*, no. 11 (about modern fakes).

Schwarz, S. (1992) 'The Sèvres porcelain service for Marie-Antoinette's dairy at Rambouillet: an exercise in archaeological Neoclassicism', *The French Porcelain Society*, no. 9, French Porcelain Society, London.

Shaw, S. (1829) *History of the Staffordshire Potteries,* Hanley (reprinted David and Charles Ltd, Newton Abbot, Devon, 1970).

Smith, L.R. (1978) *The Sydney Cove Medallion*, Wedgwood Society of Australia, Sydney.

Story, William (1861), 'Essay upon the Agriculture of Victoria', *The Victorian Government Prize Essays 1860*, George Ferres, Govt Printer, Melbourne.

Stretton, E.N. (1970) 'Early Sadler prints on Wedgwood creamware', *Proceedings of the Wedgwood Society*, no. 8, pp. 224–31.

Tait, H. (1986) 'The "Etruscan Service" of King Ferdinand IV and Josiah Wedgwood', *Ars Ceramica*, no. 3, pp. 31–4.

Towner, D. (1978) *Creamware*, Faber & Faber, London.

Watson, O. (1990) *British Studio Pottery: The Victoria and Albert Museum Collection*, Phaidon/Christie's, Oxford, in association with The Victoria and Albert Museum, London.

Wedgwood: the Australian heritage (exh. cat.), (1987) Wedgwood Australia Ltd, at David Jones, Sydney.

Wedgwood, Hensleigh C. (1981) 'The Contributions of Norman Wilson to the modernization of Wedgwood in the twentieth century', *Proceedings of the Twenty-sixth Annual Wedgwood International Seminar*, pp. 160–73.

Wedgwood & Bentley (1779) *A Catalogue*, London (reprinted The Wedgwood Society of New York, 1965).

Wedgwood & Bentley (87) *A Catalogue*, Etruria (reprinted The Wedgwood Society of New York, 1980).

Wills, G. (1980) *Wedgwood*, Country Life Books, London.

Note on perodicals

Ars Ceramica is published by the Wedgwood Society of New York.

Proceedings of the Wedgwood International Seminar is published by the Wedgwood International Seminar Inc., New York.

Proceedings of the Wedgwood Society is published by the Wedgwood Society, London.